International Customary Law and Codification

H. W. A. THIRLWAY

M. A., Ll. B. (Cantab.); Dr. en droit (Nancy); Solicitor (Hons.);
Secretary, International Court of Justice

International Customary Law and Codification

An examination of the
continuing role of custom in the present period of
codification of international law

THIS WORK WAS AWARDED THE JOHN WESTLAKE PRIZE
(1971) OF THE INSTITUT DE DROIT INTERNATIONAL

A.W. Sijthoff – Leiden 1972

ISBN 90 286 0082 5

Library of Congress Catalog Card Number: 72-76420

Printed in the Netherlands

To all those
from whom I have learned,
in gratitude

CONTENTS

FOREWORD

In January 1968, the Bureau of the Institut de droit international set as subject for the John Westlake Prize (one of the prizes founded by the late James Brown Scott) "La place que conserve la coutume dans la période actuelle de codification du droit international". The present work was completed in December 1970 and submitted as an entry for the prize; and at the Zagreb session of the Institut in August-September 1971, on the recommendation of the Jury set up for the purpose of scrutinising entries (H.E. Judge Sir Gerald Fitzmaurice, Q.C., G.C.M.G., Professor Max Sørensen, and Professor Gregory Tunkin), it was awarded the Prize.

In accordance with the Institut's Regulations governing the Prizes founded by James Brown Scott, the work is here published as it was submitted, save for certain modifications approved by the President of the Jury and the Secretary-General of the Institut, all of which are indicated in the text by square brackets, thus: [new text]. A number of additional bibliographical references have been added, and certain points have been clarified by the addition of a paragraph or two of additional argument; the major additions have however been made to take account of some of the most recent writing on the subject, e.g. Professor d'Amato's book, "The Concept of Custom in International Law", and an important paper contributed by Professor Zemanek to the *Festschrift Verdross,* entitled "Die Bedeutung der Kodifizierung des Völkerrechts für seine Anwendung". All the changes made in the text since it was submitted to the Institut are by way of addition; except for a few words here and there, deleted for stylistic reasons, nothing has been omitted.

In view of my position as an official of the Registry of the International Court of Justice, I should make it quite clear, first that the views which I have expressed are purely personal, and cannot of course be taken as having the approval of the International Court of Justice, or of the Registrar; and secondly that my comments on the Judgments and Advisory Opinions of the Court are based solely on published material, and not on any information of a confidential character to which I may have had access in the course of my duties. Accordingly, any comments of mine on the significance of any particular decision, or of any particular form of words in a Judgment, Advisory Opinion, or Separate or Dissenting Opinion, carry no more weight than those of any other student of the jurisprudence of the Court.

While my study of this subject, and the writing of the present work, has had to be done in my spare time, I have had invaluable assistance from the staff of the Court's Library, who have produced the most unlikely books and periodicals practically within instants of my asking for them, and have also drawn my attention from time to time to recent publications in this field; my debt to them is considerable. I am also happy to have the opportunity of thanking the Registrar, Dr. S.R.A. Aquarone, and the Deputy-Registrar, Mr. W. Tait, for their encouragement in what has proved to be an unexpectedly successful enterprise. Finally, it is impossible for me to express how much I owe to the unfailing support of my wife.

The Hague, October 1971 H.W.A.T.

In accordance with Article 19 of the Regulations governing the award of the Prizes founded by James Brown Scott in memory of his mother and of his sister Jeanette Scott, the undersigned Secretary-General of the *Institut de droit international* hereby declares that the present work reproduces the complete text of the paper submitted to the Institut in December 1970 and in respect of which the Institut awarded the John Westlake Prize, 1971, to its author, without modifications other than those, indicated in the text, which have been duly approved by the said Secretary-General and by the Chairman of the Jury of the Institut which recommended the award of the said Prize.

Brussels, November 6th 1971, *(sgd)* P. de Visscher

(Paul de Visscher)

Secrétaire-général de l'Institut
de droit international.

LIST OF ABBREVIATIONS

A.J.I.L.	American Journal of International Law
Annuaire français	Annuaire français de droit international
B.Y.I.L.	British Yearbook of International Law
Cal. L.R.	California Law Review
I.C.J.	International Court of Justice
I.C.L.Q.	International and Comparative Law Quarterly
I.L.C.	International Law Commission
Nederlands Tijdschrift	Nederlands Tijdschrift voor Internationaal Recht
Öst. Ztschr. für Öff. Recht	Österreichische Zeitschrift für Öffentliches Recht
P.C.I.J.	Permanent Court of International Justice
Recueil des Cours	Recueil des Cours de l'Académie de Droit International
R.G.D.I.P.	Revue générale de droit international public
Rivista	Rivista di diritto internazionale
U.N.R.I.A.A.	United Nations Reports of International Arbitral Awards
Zeitschrift	Zeitschrift für ausländisches öffentliches Recht und Völkerrecht.

Chapter One

THE MOVEMENT TOWARDS AN INTERNATIONAL *LEX SCRIPTA*

It has become a truism to observe that the community of States and other international entities whose relationships it is the task of international law to regulate, has changed radically not merely since the turn of the century, but even since the end of the Second World War. The fact that it is necessary to refer to other international entities alongside States as subjects of international law is itself a sign of an important development;[1] and even with regard merely to States, it must be remembered that they have multiplied exceedingly. Largely as a result of this multiplication, the extent of the shared aims and principles which are essential to make any sort of community out of an assemblage of free and sovereign States, has shrunk, in some instances to an alarming degree. Nor is the nature of Statehood itself the same, despite the survival of the concept of sovereignty: for example, the general prohibition of resort to force of arms in the United Nations Charter has considerably restricted the classical *jus belli et pacis.*[2] In addition, the creation of the United Nations, whether it be regarded optimistically as practically a world Parliament, with increasing legislative powers, or as something between a standing diplomatic conference and a mere sounding board, has given a new slant to political relationships, and through political relationships, to legal ones.

A community which is changing and developing at a great rate will normally need a system of law which is capable of changing or being changed or adapted almost as rapidly – "almost", because it is generally desirable that the law should lag slightly behind rather than that it should over-reach itself trying to keep up with what

1. Cf. Lauterpacht, *Collected Papers* (Cambridge 1970), Vol. I., pp. 470-471.

2. See R.Y. Jennings, The Progress of International Law, 34 *B.Y.I.L.* (1958) at pp. 338-339. Cf. also M. Lachs, Recognition and Modern Methods of International Co-operation, 35 *B.Y.I.L.* (1959), p. 252 at p. 259.

may prove to be ephemeral changes. From this point of view, custom, which while it may not be the ultimate source of law, is still the most basic source of rules to govern the activities of States, as opposed to general principles from which rules must, as a separate operation, be derived,[3] has the obvious disadvantage that it cannot, however great the need, be altered by a stroke of the pen to fit a radically altered situation. This is not to say that customary law cannot, in the circumstances of today, change and develop very much more rapidly than was the case in the smaller and in a sense less active international community of the last century;[4] for while the existence of a larger body of States may make the achievement of a general consensus of views on a point more difficult to achieve, it does at the same time make it likely that there will be more frequent acts by States which will contribute to the formation of a usage, particularly in a world where States are in more continuous and more varied relationships with each other than ever before. None the less, customary international law is something which develops at a pace which, for being sure, tends to be majestic.

As a result, new developments in such fields as, for example, the techniques of overseas investment may find customary law insufficient to give full effect to the rights and duties of the parties as one or both of them understand them: thus in the recent Judgment of the International Court of Justice in the *Barcelona Traction* case,[5] the Court, after ruling that no existing rule of customary law conferred on the national State of shareholders in a company a right of action on the international level in respect of injury done to the company, observed that

> "... in the present state of the law, the protection of shareholders requires that recourse be had to be treaty stipulations or special agreements directly concluded between the private investor and the State in which the investment is placed".[6]

---

3. For the concept of general principles as the "real source" of law, as opposed to custom and treaty as "formal sources", see Accioly, *Tratado de direito internacional publico* (Rio de Janeiro, 1956), p. 33.

4. "... the speedy tempo of present international life promoted by highly developed communication ... had minimized the importance of the time factor and has made possible the acceleration of the formation of customary international law. What required a hundred years in former days now may require less than ten years." Dissenting opinion of Judge Tanaka, *Continental Shelf* cases, *I.C.J. Reports 1969*, p. 171, at p. 177.

5. *I.C.J. Reports 1970*, p. 3.

6. *Ibid.*, p. 47, para. 90.

As Judge Sir Gerald Fitzmaurice remarked in his separate opinion,

> "the results to which a strict view of the law leads – as it stands *de lege lata* – are not satisfactory",[7]

and the root cause of the unsatisfactory results was that the Belgian Government was playing the role of a pioneer in a field in which the melancholy task of the pioneer is to contribute to the formation of law which he cannot himself invoke. The Court dismissed the case – as, it is submitted, it was bound to do – on the ground that Belgium's claim, however morally justified, was without precedent in customary international law.

Another recent case before the International Court, which we will have to study from several points of view, may be said to illustrate the impact on traditional law of technological advances. Twenty years ago, the exploitation of the continental shelf had barely begun: today it is of considerable economic importance to the whole world. The labours of the International Law Commission, which culminated in the 1958 Geneva Convention on the Continental Shelf, laid down a régime which was generally acceptable and appeared to have a solid legal foundation: but in the *North Sea Continental Shelf* cases in 1969, between States one of which was not a party to the Convention, the International Court could not uphold that régime as customary law without doing violence to the concept of the formation of customary law.[8]

The law of the continental shelf is, in any sense, new law;[9] but even in the traditional fields of law – the classic sub-divisions of textbooks – a surprising amount of law is incomplete and unsystematic.[10] Law which develops inductively, as it were, from practice, shares – to a great extent – with law developing from decided cases the disadvantage of leaving apparent gaps at points where no practice has occurred to give expression to such rules as might be found appropriate. While the practical importance of this may, as we shall see,[11] be exaggerated, it is none the less more than a purely academic problem.

7. *Ibid.*, p. 84.

8. *I.C.J. Reports 1969*, p. 3, particularly pp. 41-45.

9. In the view of Professor François, it is a fundamental mistake to regard the law of the continental shelf as customary law, rather than as a developing treaty régime based on general principles of law. J.P.A. François, *Grondlijnen van het Volkenrecht* (Zwolle, 1967, p. 346).

10. See Lauterpacht in 49 *A.J.I.L.* (1955), p. 17.

11. See below, pp. 22-23.

A further factor adverse to the efficient operation of traditional customary law is the rapid increase in the number of States and of international organisations of one sort or another, which are also increasingly recognised as subjects of international law. In the first place, since the existence, and even more the establishment of the observed existence, of a customary rule of international law depends on the presence of a large measure of agreement [or identity of approach] among States, the widening of the international community increases the difficulty of ascertaining what are the undoubted rules of law, even though the contribution of the new States will normally be limited to admitting or contesting the relevance of practices in which they themselves took no part.

Secondly, the fragmentation of territorial entities, coupled with present-day political conditions, encourages the trend toward regionalization in organization, and in political and legal philosophy, among those called upon to direct the foreign affairs of States. The growth of a regional law of the Americas, fostered by the Organization of American States, is likely to be paralleled by the growth of a regional law of Africa under the umbrella of the Organization of African Unity,[12] even though the difficulties resulting from wider diversities of indigenous cultures, and the presence of two major imported languages and legal systems, is likely to act to some extent as a brake on this process. It would not seem difficult to imagine a world of the future in which customary law would have become splintered into systems of regional customary law, linked only by general treaties, the UN charter, and a growing body of "United Nations law" deriving its force ultimately from the Charter, though this does not seem imminent at present.

Thirdly by far the largest number of new States are emerging from a situation of dependence, which tends to be classified in retrospect as subjection, with regard to one or more of the older States. However difficult it may be to reconcile with what is, after all, the self-evident principle of the universality of international law,[13] the claim of such new States to reject certain aspects of traditional law which are distasteful as smacking of colonialism is understandable, and may in practice prove difficult to resist. The legal basis for such claims usually advanced is essentially a volun-

12. Cf. Ammoun, *I.C.J. Reports 1970*, p. 290, para. 5.
13. See, for example, Fitzmaurice in 92 Recueil des Cours. 1957 – II, pp. 95ff.

tarist position: new States, it is said, are not necessarily bound by rules of general international law in the elaboration of which, by accumulation of usage, the new States took no part.[14] This is of course not an argument which can be set up against such treaties as the new State may have been prevailed upon to undertake at the time of its creation, or subsequently, and while the *clausula rebus sic stantibus* may have its uses, and despite the resurgence of the doctrine, so carefully expelled in the time of Vattel,[15] of the vitiating effect on treaties of duress,[16] it is in general more difficult to justify the abandonment of treaty obligations than a refusal to accept principles of customary law.

The impact of the emergence of new States, and of the attitude of many them to traditional law, makes itself felt in two ways, both inimical to the force and progress of custom as a source of law. First, it is reasonable to expect that when granting independence to, or entering into relations with, a new State of this type, it may well be felt to be wiser to enter into express treaty relationships rather than rely on what might otherwise have been regarded as well-established rules of customary law; and thus the dissent of new States, however unjustified in theory, will inevitably operate to weaken the authority of customary law in general, even among States of the older international community, and may in fact come to achieve the disappearance or amendment of the rules dissented from.[17]

Secondly, the new States themselves are in many cases anxious to cause their own views of international law to prevail, not merely with regard to matters which were formerly regulated by customary law rules which they are anxious to see discarded, but

14. Cf. [Tunkin, Remarks on the Juridical Nature of Customary Norms of International Law, 49 *Cal. L.R.,* (1961) p. 419 at p. 428;] Separate Opinion of Judge Ammoun, *Barcelona Traction Light & Power Company Limited, I.C.J. Reports 1970,* pp. 329-330.

15. Cf. Vattel, *Droit des Gens,* ed. Pradier Fodéré (1863), II, p. 147.

16. See Vienna Convention on the Law of Treaties, art. 52. Cf. Ammoun, *ibid.,* p. 309.

17. "Nel mentre si contesta quindi che i nuovi Stati possano, al momento in cui divengono membri della comunità internazionale, scegliere quali sono le norme che vogliono rispettare e indicare quelle alle quali non intendono invece ottemperare – non si esclude la possibilità che l'ammissione nella comunità internazionale di un numero massiccio di nuovi Stati che si oppongono a determinate norme di diritto internazionale consuetudinario possa portare eventualmente alla modificazione o abrogazione di queste." Sereni, I Nuovi Stati ed il Diritto internazionale, 50 *Rivista* (1967), pp. 14-15.

also by the establishment of new principles of particular interest to formerly dependent – and economically still insecure – territories. The creation of new rules of customary law, even when there is from the outset little disagreement as to their desirability is, as we have seen, a slow process; and to appeal to custom to attempt to impose upon the "old" States rules which they may be disinclined to accept is hardly consistent with the discarding of "old" customary rules unacceptable to "new" States.[18] Thus, it is natural to turn to some form of codification, or legislation, so far as such a thing exists, and to enshrine the desired principles not merely in treaties – which have to be expressly accepted – but in resolutions and declarations, purporting to be a new *lex scripta,* of universal authority. The General Assembly of the United Nations, in which the Afro-Asian States can now easily summon a majority, has inevitably served this purpose, and the quantity and scope of "law-making" resolutions is impressive, whatever qualitative effect one is prepared to attribute to them.[19]

Thus concern for a system of law fully adapted to the present day, and even for a system of law of which a principal virtue would be its newness – new law for new States – has led to a movement towards the treaty, and in particular the codifying

18. On this, and on the impact of the "new" States on international law in general, see the article of Professor L.C. Green in 74 *R.G.D.I.P.* (1970), pp. 78-106. See also the article of Sereni in 72 *R.G.D.I.P.* (1968) p. 305, and the bibliography there given.

19. [The resolutions in the following list (which is not exhaustive) have all been claimed to have law-making or law-declaring effect:

General Assembly resolution 95 (I) approving the principles of international law embodied in the Charter of the Nuremberg Tribunal;

Universal Declaration of Human Rights, G.A. resolution 217 (III), 10 December 1948;

Declaration of the Rights of the Child, G.A. resolution 1386 (XIV), 20 November 1959;

Declaration on the Granting or independence to Colonial Countries and Peoples, G.A. resolution 1514 (XV), 14 December 1960;

Declaration on the Prohibition of the Use of Nuclear and Thermo-Nuclear Weapons, G.A. resolution 1653 (XVI), 24 November 1961;

Declarations of Legal Principles Governing the Activities of States in the Exploration and Use of Outer Space, G.A. resolution 1721 (XVI), 20 December 1961 and G.A. resolution 1962 (XVIII), 13 December 1963;

Declaration on Permanent Sovereignty over Natural Wealth and Resources, G.A. resolution 1803 (XVII), 14 December 1962;

Declaration on the Elimination of all Forms of Racial Discrimination, G.A. resolution 1904 (XVIII), 20 November 1963;

Declaration of Principles of International Law Concerning Friendly Relations and Co-operation between States, G.A. resolution 2625 (XXV), 24 October 1970.]

treaty, as the prime source of law, and the principal method for its development. There are other factors; for example, certain aspects of the international community founded upon the UN Charter tend towards the same result.

A particular feature of the post-war period has been the encroachment of international lawmaking activity on the reserved domain of States, a process which has come to pose a problem of method, and to justify techniques which may prove an embarrassing precedent in the future.

The right of a State to respect for its sovereignty in the form of abstention by other States and organizations from interference in matters falling within its domestic jurisdiction, expressly preserved in Article 2, paragraph 7, of the UN Charter, is a creature of custom, and has always been subject first to limitation by treaty,[20] and secondly, to actual or potential narrowing-down by the growth of new practice, recognized as belonging to customary international law, and operating to restrict the operation of basic principle. But the kernel of the matter – the relationship of a State with its own subjects – has been generally immune from the impact of developing customary law, for a very simple reason. Custom derives from the *de facto* adjustment of conflicting claims and interests of the subjects of international law; and it has always been – and probably still is – one of the most fundamental tenets of international law that individuals and private corporations are not subjects of international law. The relationship between a State and an individual cannot be creative of international custom, even if the individual enjoys the protection of another State:[21] what may be creative of customary law is the relationship between a State which has acted in a certain way towards an individual and another State to which that individual is linked by a bond recognized by international law as sufficient to entitle the State to press an international claim which, while it may be effectively for the redress of the wrongs of the individual, is in law for redress of the wrongs of the claimant State.[22] Where the individual concerned is the national of the State whose action is complained of, the

20. The right of a State to impose limitations on its own sovereignty is, as the P.C.I.J. pointed out in the *Wimbledon* case, itself an attribute of sovereignty.

21. Contra, Lauterpacht, *International Law and Human Rights,* p. 27; see the criticism of this view by Waldock, 106 *Recueil des Cours,* 1962-II, pp. 192-19.

22. The classic statement of the principle is of course that of the P.C.I.J. in the *Chorzów Factory* case, *P.C.I.J. Series A, No. 17,* at p. 28.

essentially bilateral nature of the relationship required for the application and development of international customary law is not present, and whatever treatment is inflicted by the State on the individual is *res inter alios acta.*[23]

Thus it is not strictly accurate to refer, as a matter of international law, to a State having a right to act as it pleases with regard to its own subjects, since to assert the existence of a right is also to assert the obligation of other subjects of the legal system within which the right is claimed to respect the right. This may be demonstrated by postulating the case of a claim by the UN for reparation for injury to an official, for which the official's own national State was responsible: the claim could not be denied in the name of a "right" to treat the official as the State pleased. Until the present century at least, it was generally true to say that States did not restrain other States from action directed to the nationals of the State concerned;[24] but this was not because they were under any obligation to respect a right in the State concerned, but because there was normally no incentive for them to do so, and more fundamentally, because in doing so they would be not only asserting the entry of the individual into the legal order in which they themselves existed, but also claiming a right to press the claim of the individual, as opposed to a claim of their own. The decision of the I.C.J. in the *Nottebohm* case[25] shows how the whole trend of customary law is opposed to such a development.

This is not to say that it is impossible for international law to take cognisance of the general relationships between a State and its own subjects, but merely that the only effective technique by which such relationships could become an element within the international legal system was that of the treaty.[26] There is of course no objection of principle to a State binding itself by treaty

23. [Cf. d'Amato: "[it is] a basic fact of international life that whenever any state claims a freedom to act, its act is impinging in some way upon the freedom of another state or of the general body of states. If this were not so –if, for instance, the issue was one arising solely within the domestic jurisdiction of a state – then by definition international law would not be involved" (The Authoritativeness of Custom in International Law, 53 *Rivista,* p. 491 at p. 501)].

24. A few exceptions are mentioned by Waldock, 106 *Recueil des Cours* 1962-II, p. 196; see also Ermacora, Human Rights and Domestic Jurisdiction, 124 *Recueil des Cours,* 1968-II, p. 371.

25. *I.C.J. Reports 1955,* p. 4.

26. Cf. the Resolution of the Institut de droit international of 29 april 1954 on the determination of the reserved domain, Articles 3 and 5 (Annuaire, 1954, t. II, p. 300).

with another subject of international law to observe a certain conduct towards its own subjects, or a certain class of them, although such a treaty operates to reduce the reserved domain of that State; such a treaty creates a link between the individuals concerned and the entity with which the treaty is concluded, analogous to the link of nationality justifying diplomatic protection. An excellent example of this technique is of course afforded by the Minorities Treaties concluded as part of the settlement after the First World War, which gave the Permanent Court of International Justice so much employment during the 1920's and early 1930's.[27]

It may be objected that the "functional" right of protection by the United Nations of its agents constitutes, in the hypothetical case postulated above, an example of encroachment on the reserved domain by the growth of customary law; particularly since the International Court, in its Advisory Opinion on the question, did not regard the right of protection as exercisable only against Member-States.[28] In fact, the right in question was derived, in the Court's reasoning, ultimately from the Charter, and had become extended as a consequence of the international personality of the United Nations. Furthermore, the Court emphasized that the right asserted by the Organization is its own right, not that of its agent.[29]

With the conclusion of the Charter of the United Nations, which included in its purposes and principles the avowed aim of achieving "international co-operation in . . . promoting and encouraging respect for human rights and for fundamental freedoms for all", the relevance of the individual in international law took on a new significance. The treaty, and in particular the multilateral treaty, was clearly the principal instrument for achieving international co-operation, particularly in this field, but the preparation and the bringing into force of multilateral treaties, even on questions not related to so tender a point as a State's relationship with its subjects, is not something which can be achieved without long delay and many disappointments and compromises.[30] From

27. Kunz has suggested that the modern emphasis on Human Rights is merely a new "fashion", the concept of protection of minorities being the former "fashion". See 48 *A.J.I.L.* (1954), p. 282.

28. *I.C.J. Reports 1949*, p. 171 at pp. 184-185.

29. *Ibid.*, at pp. 181-184.

30. See below, pp. 103-104.

this point of view, the adoption by the General Assembly of the Universal Declaration of Human Rights on 10 December 1948,[31] as a statement of an ideal to be achieved, was undoubtedly a contribution to progress; but from the point of view of the technique of development of international law, it was less fortunate. Such declarations commit no State to any precise action; but at the same time, they serve as a very handy stick to beat a political adversary with, particularly if they can be, for the occasion, attributed the force of international law.

It would undoubtedly be an excellent thing if the principles of the Universal Declaration of Human Rights were to pass into international law, although it could not do so to any real effect unless it were accompanied by the establishment of procedure to render it effective;[32] but for that very reason, it is not possible for it to become part of customary international law.[33] If an individual complains that his own national State has infringed the rights which the Declaration seeks to guarantee to him, his complaint is doomed to remain in the wilderness outside the pale of international law so long as there is no international legal entity which can espouse it and so bring it into international existence.

Faced with this difficulty and with the disappointing slowness in the implementation of any more effective texts, it is understandable that some writers should have argued in favour of the entry of principles into general international law by some process

31. [G.A. resolution 217 (III)].

32. "... on the universal level, the instruments which embody human rights do not confer on States the capacity to protect the victims of infringement of such rights irrespective of their nationality" *Barcelona Traction, I.C.J. Reports 1970*, p. 47, para. 91. It is arguable that an effect of the Declaration is to extend the generally recognised right of diplomatic protection to all breaches of the Declaration committed against a national of the protecting State; but this is virtually incapable of proof, because such a breach will almost certainly be an international tort apart from the provisions of the Declaration.

33. Contra, R.Y. Jennings, The Progress of International Law, 34 *B.Y.I.L.* (1958) who speaks of the "rapidly developing *customary* and conventional law of human rights, which affects the State's treatment of its own subjects"; [Vice-President Ammoun in *Legal Consequences for States of the Continued Presence of South Africa in Namibia (South West Africa), I.C.J. Reports 1971*, p. 76: "the affirmations of the Declaration ... can bind States on the basis of custom within the meaning of paragraph 1 (b) of [Article 38 of the Court's Statute], whether because they constituted a codification of customary law ... or because they have acquired the force of custom through a general practice accepted as law ..." Cf. also Stefan Glaser, Les droits de l'homme à la lumière du droit international positif, in *Mélanges Rolin*, p. 104.]

which either by-passes or assumes the consent of States. It is legitimate to point to the fact that the Declaration was adopted without a dissenting vote (though with abstentions) among the States then Members of the United Nations, and that no State which has subsequently become a member of the Organization has denounced or objected to the principles set out in the Declaration as such. In view of the reference to human rights in the Charter, quoted above, it is also possible to regard Declarations of this kind as forms of interpretation of the Charter, which are therefore binding as treaty-law as being part of the Charter, though this view comes up against formidable difficulties, discussion of which is somewhat outside the scope of the questions here examined.

But, for reasons to be examined below,[34] it is not possible to regard the Declaration of Human Rights, or subsequent General Assembly Declarations of similar scope and purpose, either as declaratory of existing customary law, or as statements of principles which have subsequently passed into customary law, without adopting a concept of the nature of customary law and the way in which it comes into existence which is radically different from the traditional concept.

A further aspect of the movement towards an international *lex scripta* which should be noted is its impact on the decisions of international tribunals as a source of law. The example of the 1969 Vienna Convention on the Law of Treaties will serve to draw attention to what may prove an unexpected and unfortunate side-effect of the codification drive which we are witnessing.

It is well known that in the post-war period, continuous and increasing difficulty has been encountered in the preparation of multilateral treaties with regard to the provision to be made in such treaties for the settlement of disputes arising out of the interpretation or application of the provisions of the treaty. Originally largely attributable to the influence of Soviet legal thinking, in which the conception of the rule of law as requiring the judgments of a competent tribunal to be binding on all, including the State itself, has proved unacceptable,[35] the difficulty is now reinforced by the generally suspicious attitude of many of the new States toward the International Court of

34. See p. 67ff.

35. On the Soviet attitude to the settlement of disputes through international tribunals, see Grzybowski, *Soviet Public International Law* (1970), pp. 457ff.

Justice,[36] which is of course the tribunal to which disputes on the interpretation or application of a treaty should, if possible, be referred in all cases.[37]

It is for this reason that what should have become practically the *clause de style* in treaties of this type, namely the clause conferring jurisdiction on the International Court of Justice for disputes between parties to the Treaty on its interpretation or application, the clause itself constituting acceptance of jurisdiction, and not amounting merely to a *pactum de contrahendo,* has had to be transferred, only too frequently, to a separate Optional Protocol.[38]

In the 1969 Vienna Convention, however, this process has gone a step further. While the jurisdiction of the Court is preserved insofar as disputes concerning matters of *jus cogens* is concerned (Articles 53, 64 and 66 of the Convention), for all other disputes a special procedure of conciliation is provided (Article 66(b) and Annex to the Convention).

This is not merely a failure to advance: it is in fact a retrograde step in relation to the jurisdiction of the International Court.[39] The system of the optional protocol was never likely to extend the Court's jurisdiction to many States which were otherwise cool towards it, although it was more to be expected that a State would, when adopting the principal treaty, adopt the Optional Protocol, than that such State would deposit an acceptance of jurisdiction generally under the "optional clause" in the Court's Statute, and so such States might come to move by gentle steps towards a more general acceptance of jurisdiction. For the wooing of such States, the terms of the Vienna Convention lend no assistance.

On the other hand, many of the States which participated in the work of the Vienna Conference, and are likely to become parties

36. Cf. Jenks, *The Prospects of International Adjucation,* p. 105.

37. See the model Clause proposal by the Institut de droit international, *Annuaire* 1956, p. 365.

38. E.g. the Optional Protocols to the Vienna Conventions on Diplomatic Relations and on Consular Relations.

39. It is clear from the records and observers' accounts of the Vienna Conference that the provision in question was a compromise clause which satisfied no-one, but which was the most that could be achieved in view of the stand taken by certain groups of States. See, for example, Briggs, Reflections on the Codification of International Law by the International Law Commission and by Other Agencies, 126 Recueil des Cours, 1969-I, at pp. 302ff.; [Dupuy, Codification et règlement des différends: les débats de Vienne sur les procédures de règlement, *Annuaire français* 1969, p. 70.]

to the Convention, have either deposited acceptances of jurisdiction under the "optional clause", or are linked to other States by general treaties for the settlement of disputes, which provide for the jurisdiction of the International Court of Justice. In such acceptances, and in such treaties, a common exception or reservation is the exclusion of disputes which the parties have agreed to settle in some other way.[40] Thus the provisions in the Vienna Convention will operate, so far as such States are concerned, not merely not to increase the role of the International Court, but actively to decrease it. However sympathetic States may be to international judicial settlement in general, their ardour is likely to cool at the door of the courtroom, so that even the commencement of proceedings tends to be regarded as an unfriendly act.[41] It is therefore unrealistic to hope that the existence of a general settlement treaty or an acceptance of jurisdiction will mean that the States concerned will waive the objection that the Vienna Convention provides for a different form of settlement, and choose litigation rather than non-binding conciliation, however suited to judicial settlement the subject of the dispute may be.

For this reason, it is to be hoped that the precedent of Article 66 of the Vienna Convention on the Law of Treaties will not be followed; but it cannot be denied that the present climate of opinion in the United Nations and elsewhere is not favourable to the settlement of disputes of this kind by the International Court of Justice.

There is however a more recent variant of the disputes clause conferring jurisdiction on the International Court of Justice which is very much to be preferred; it was used in the Tokyo Convention on Offences and Certain Other Acts Committed on board Aircraft,[42] and most recently in the I.C.A.O. Convention on the same subject drafted at The Hague at the beginning of December 1970. The relevant clause in the latter Convention reads as follows: –

> "1. Any dispute between two or more Contracting States concerning the interpretation or application of this Convention which cannot be settled through negotiation, shall, at the request of one of them, be submitted to arbitration. If within six months from the date of the request for arbitration the Parties are

---

40. See, in *I.C.J. Yearbook 1970/1971*, e.g. acceptances of jurisdiction by Australia (p. 44), France (p. 52), and Israel (p. 55).

41. Cf. the discussions of the Institut de Droit International in 1954, and the Model Clause adopted on 17 April 1956, *Annuaire* 1956, p. 365

42. *International Legal Materials,* 1963, p. 1042, at p. 1045.

unable to agree on the organisation of the arbitration, any one of those Parties may refer the dispute to the International Court of Justice by request in conformity with the Statute of the Court.

2. Each State may at the time of signature or ratification of this Convention or accession thereto, declare that it does not consider itself bound by the preceding paragraph. The other Contracting States shall not be bound by the preceding paragraph with respect to any Contracting State having made such a reservation.

3. Any Contracting State having made a reservation in accordance with the preceding paragraph may at any time withdraw this reservation by notification to the Depositary Governments"[43]

The virtue of this clause is that it does not, as the clause in the Vienna Convention does, interfere with the existing broad grouping of States which are sympathetic to the concept of international judicial settlement and those which are not. The latter may be expected to make a reservation to the clause; but the former, and with them many States which have no very definite position on the point, will be linked by the clause with a kind of compulsory jurisdiction. The clause is therefore also preferable to the former system of optional protocols and it is to be hoped that it will be followed in future.

These tendencies in general adverse to the jurisdiction of the International Court of Justice are not regrettable merely because they leave open the question of how any final settlement of disputes is to be achived if negotiations, conciliation etc., are ineffective, but also because international judicial settlement is itself an important factor in the growth of law, and its adaptation to changing conditions.[44] This is a subject to which we shall return; but it may be observed here that it may well prove short-sighted to seek to regulate legal relationships by agreement in advance, as it were, through the medium of codifying treaties, and at the same time to discount the value of impartial settlement of the disputes to which any such instrument is almost bound to give rise.

Before proceeding further with our study, we should note one other important influence contributing to the trend towards *lex scripta*, and add a clarification of the scope of our discussion.

43. I.C.A.O. Conference documents SA Doc. No. 80: Article 12 of the Convention as adopted.

44. See Lauterpacht, *The Development of International Law by the International Court, passim*; Zafrulla Khan, The Contribution of the Principal Judicial Organ of the United Nations to the Achievement of the Objectives of the Organisation, *UN Monthly Chronicle,* July 1970.

The law of the present age is strongly marked by the advances of technology in the last half-century, not merely in matters of general law, such as that of outer space, or the bed of the ocean,[45] but also inasmuch as it has become necessary to conclude international agreements to settle innumerable details of such relationships as those involved in postal communications. It must be conceded that this is a field where it is essential to have recourse to written agreements, regulations and codes, and the role of custom must necessarily be extremely limited.

For this reason, in our discussions of the relationships of customary international law and codifying instruments, we are not concerned with instruments of the detailed kind just referred to which – however vital they may be to the relations of States – do not present problems of particular interest from the point of view of the theoretical lawyer.[46]

45. See Mouton, The Impact of Science on International Law, 119 *Recueil des cours,* 1966-III, 183.

46. Cf. Jenks, The Conflict of Law-Making Treaties, 30 *B.Y.I.L.* (1953) p. 401: an attitude of detachment "is an understandable reaction to a complex body of detailed rules, many of them dealing with matters of a highly technical character, which do not afford the same scope as the common law for the development of legal principle by argument from precedent".

Chapter Two

CONCEPTS AND METHODS OF CODIFICATION OF INTERNATIONAL LAW

Up to this point, in discussing the trend towards an international *lex scripta*, we have treated the codification of international law rather as something which has come to exist, for the reasons discussed in the previous chapter, and which may be taken for granted. Before proceeding further, we should make a closer examination of what is meant by codification in this field, and of the techniques by which it may be effected.

[To avoid any possibility of confusion, it may be as well to make it clear from the outset that codification of private international law is excluded from the scope of the present study, since private international law is by definition no part of customary international law. The point may seem too obvious for mention; but since codification of private international law is effected, in the sense we are considering, by international treaty, the codification partakes of the nature of public international law to that extent; and when examining, for example, the question of succession to codifying treaties,[1] it is essential for our purposes to put on one side treaties codifying private international law, since wholly different considerations apply to them.[2]]

In his Dictionnaire de la terminologie du droit international,[3] Basdevant distinguishes two main meanings of the term "Codification du droit international", one of which he finds it necessary to sub-divide into three subsidiary concepts. One of the two main meanings he records need not detain us long: this is what Reuter[4] distinguishes as "codification scientifique", as opposed to "codi-

1. [See below, pp. 143-4.]

2. [See generally Vitta, International Conventions and National Conflict Systems, 126 *Recueil des Cours,* 1969-I, p. 111.]

3. Paris, Sirey, 1960; p. 120.

4. Reuter, Institutions Internationales, p. 158; [The same term is used by Ago, La codification du droit international, *En hommage à Paul Guggenheim,* p. 93 at p. 98.]

fication juridique", namely the preparation of unofficial codes of existing or desirable law by scholars acting as scholars and not as representatives of any State or group of States.[5] Whatever the value as persuasive authority of such "restatements" (to adopt the convenient American term), for example as evidence of the *opinio juris*, they can clearly only influence the development of international law to the extent that they inspire Governments either to adopt the practices proposed, so as ultimately to create new customary law, or to reproduce their provisions in codifying treaties.[6]

Dealing with "la codification juridique", Basdevant distinguishes what might be called the three stages of codification.[7] The first is "the systematic statement of rules which already exist". In this connection, Article 15 of the Statute of the International Law Commission is recalled, which reads:

> "... the expression 'codification of international law' is used for convenience as meaning the more precise formulation and systematization of rules of international law in fields where there already has been extensive State practice, precedent and doctrine."

Clearly there is already some difference between the systematic statement of rules which already exist, and the more precise formulation (not to mention "systematization",[8] which in this context could cover a wide range of adjustments of detail in established rules) of rules in fields in which there has not merely been State practice and precedent but also doctrine.[9] As has already been observed, customary law is inevitably a ragged system; but to fill in the gaps, however logically, and on the strength of whatever doctrinal authority, is going beyond the re-statement of existing law. This was pointed out by Professor Brierley at the time when the Statute was drafted.[10]

5. For South American writers, codification is the task of States alone, to be effected by "conventions or other international agreements": Moreno Quintana, *Tratado de derecho internacional*, Vol. I, p. 109. This view is obviously influenced by South American practice, the most advanced as regards regional codification.

6. Cf. Lauterpacht, Codification and Development of International Law, 49 *A.J.I.L.* (1955) p. 31.

7. Prof. François (*Handboek van het Volkenrecht*, p. 620) also gives a threefold definition, but for him the third stage is purely legislative, and an improper use of the term "codification".

8. An earlier draft had "more systematic arrangement": UN Doc. A/AC.10/SR.14, p. 8.

9. Cf. Oppenheim (8th Edn. by Lauterpacht) Vol. I, p. 52, note 1.

10. See UN Doc. A/AC.10/SR.6, pp. 3-4.

It is however generally recognised that pure re-statement of the law, where the law in question is international custom, is often hardly possible, and where possible would generally be so incomplete and fragmentary as to be of little practical use. Minor adjustments of the kind contemplated are unlikely to give rise to any problem in practice: if the result is to be a treaty, the rules which have been "added" to the pre-existing law will be binding by virtue of the treaty; and even if the codification is expressed in purely declaratory form, the whole will have the authority of those scholars who participated, as well as that of any pre-existing doctrine by which they may have been guided. If the codification is effected with the co-operation of, or at least in consultation with, representatives of the majority of States, it is likely that any objections to the "addition" will be made during the drafting process, rather than later when the question arises in practice.[11]

The second stage, and Basdevant's second definition, is that in which

> "la codification est entendue comme comportant non la simple déclaration du droit existant, mais son aménagement, son amendement, sa réforme, ses modifications et compléments suivant les exigences des rapports internationaux et sans chercher à distinguer dans le résultat de cette opération ce qui est consécration du droit existant de ce qui est innovation par rapport à celui-ci".[12]

Thus the working definition given in Article 15 of the Statute of the International Law Commission is already half way to the second "stage" of the concept of codification; and the distinction between codification and "progressive development" would be in danger of becoming blurred, were the latter term not restrictively defined in the same Article of the Commission's Statute as

> "the preparation of draft conventions on subjects which have not yet been regulated by international law or in regard to which the law has not yet been sufficiently developed in the practice of States".

The significant use of the word "sufficiently" will be noted; it is to be presumed that the meaning is "sufficiently for codification (as defined in Article 15) to be possible", though this interpreta-

11. On the possible effect of failing to mention an objection based on a claim to a special régime, note the views of Lord McNair in his dissenting opinion in the *Fisheries* Case (*I.C.J. Reports 1951*, p. 158 at p. 179) on the position of the Norwegian representative at the 1881 Hague Conference.

12. *Dictionnaire de la terminologie du droit international*, p. 122. [The term adopted for codification in this sense by Professor Ago is "codification normative": see La codification du droit international, in *En hommage à Paul Guggenheim*, p. 93, at p. 98.]

tion would be more natural if Article 15 mentioned codification before progressive development instead of the other way around, as is the case.

As Manley Hudson has observed, with reference to Article 15 of the I.L.C. Statute, "there could be no codification without development",[13] and for this reason it is suggested that it is Basdevant's second definition of "la codification juridique" which corresponds most nearly to the process which, except where an indication is clearly given that the intention is to make changes in the law, takes place when a work of codification is effected, by the International Law Commission or any other international body.[14]

The final definition noted (without comment) by Basdevant should be mentioned for the sake of completeness, although it is something of a *lusus naturae*; it has been argued by Scelle that

> "tout traité-loi normatif ou constructif, fût-il simplement bilatéral, est déjà partiellement une codification, en ce qui concerne la société interétatique particulière où il intervient".[15]

This somewhat extreme view of the law-making and codifying effects of a treaty is not germane to the present discussion. What should however be noted here is the contention of Lauterpacht that codification should and does cover also the substitution, for a generally recognised existing rule, of a wholly new rule considered by the person or body responsible for the codification as more satisfactory.[16] This process, while it is admittedly capable of being a desirable practice in some fields of law, can surely only be called "codification" by stretching that elastic term practically to breaking point.

The discussions which preceded the adoption of Article 15 of the Statute of the International Law Commission, and the Commission's own discussions of that Article in 1951, were by no means academic debates, but were related to the very practical problem of the Commission's methods of work. It had originally been suggested, by the United States delegate, that the methods

13. I.L.C., 3rd Session: *I.L.C. Yearbook 1951*, p. 123, para. 120.

14. Cf. the definition of codification given by Moreno Quintana: "la elaboración de normas jurídicas destinadas a regular la totalidad o parte del derecho internacional entre varios estados", without mention of its relationship with existing law (*Tratado de derecho internacional,* Vol. I, p. 109).

15. 46 *Recueil des Cours*, p. 465.

16. 49 *A.J.I.L.* (1955) pp. 27-29.

and procedures would vary according to whether the task was codification or development of international law,[17] and the two different methods thus postulated became equated with the use of general conventions (to be proposed by the Commission for the development of law) and of scientific restatements (for codification). This question bedevilled the discussions of the drafting Committee for some time.[18] The Russian member pressed for the use of a Convention in all cases, apparently on the basis of a particular interpretation of the term "codification", not shared by his colleagues on the committee, as covering a considerable degree of reform, if not of development.[19] The Secretariat, on the other hand, had drawn attention to the dangers,[20] involved in giving States the opportunity of challenging, on their appearance in the form of a convention, rules of law which were already generally accepted as part of general customary law, and thus causing law to take a step backwards.[21] The final version of Article 15 was, it seems, something of a compromise.

At a distance of over twenty years, and in the light of subsequent events, it may seem that the two questions, that of codification as distinct from development, and that of the use of conventions as opposed to restatements, may have become inter-related to an unnecessary degree. As already observed, pure re-statement, at the present stage of the development of international law, is not really a practical or useful possibility; and the question of method can be treated purely from the point of view of the practical merits and demerits of the methods available. A statement, not intended to be included in a treaty text, can contain provisions intended *de lege ferenda* as well as *de lege lata*, provided of course that it is made clear that this is the case, and it may still prove useful in providing, as it were, the first crystal in a solu-

17. See UN Doc. A/AC.10/11, p. 5.

18. For a study of the debates, see Briggs, *The International Law Commission*, (1965), pp. 129ff.

19. See UN Doc. A/AC.10/SR 4, p. 5, and Add. 1. Grzybowski (*Soviet Public International Law*, pp. 28-29) mentions that at the time Soviet legal thinking was opposed to the codification of international law as being tantamount to an attempt by the Western powers to preserve the *status quo* from development.

20. See "Memorandum on Methods for Encouraging the Progressive Development of International Law and its Eventual Codification" (1947) UN Doc. A/AC.10/7 Note the word "eventual"!

21. Cf. the astringent comments of Scelle, *I.L.C. Yearbook 1957*, Vol II, pp. 1-11, particularly paragraphs 7-14 (on the draft on Arbitral Procedure).

tion – put in from outside, in order to stimulate crystallisation – on which further crystals can build; i.e. it can serve to give direction and unity to subsequent practice so as to make it creative of law.

On the other hand, the fears expressed in the Memorandum of the Secretariat have to some extent been confirmed by the fate of carefully worked out international codifying instruments which, for lack of support, have been "still-born" as Charles de Visscher has expressed it.[22]

From what has been said as to the meaning of the term codification as applied to international law, it will be clear that for codification to be a reasonable proposition, the existence of at least a certain amount of customary law in the field to be covered is normally necessary. Opinions may differ as to whether the term "ripe for codification" really means anything;[23] but if there is no law in the field, or if there is a complete system of law which is to be altered, then as we have seen, the word codification has to be stretched fairly energetically to cover the process contemplated. This question of the relationship to codification of the pre-existing customary law was examined by the late Sir Hersch Lauterpacht in 1955 in an important article, to which reference has already been made.[24] Lauterpacht was a strong supporter of the codification process in international law, and several of the stimulating observations made in that article merit some examination here.

Lauterpacht first drew attention to the very considerable lack of agreed existing law which becomes apparent once any particular field is examined with the closeness required by the preparation of proposals for codification.

> "... once we approach at close quarters practically any branch of international law, we are driven, amidst some feeling of incredulity, to the conclusion that although there is as a rule a consensus of opinion on broad principle ... there is no semblance of agreement in relation to specific rules and problems".[25]

Insofar as this observation relates to an absence of clearly-established law, as distinct from the existence of competing schools of thought as to specific rules, it will perhaps come as less of a surprise to those who have become accustomed to stumbling on

22. *Théories et réalités en droit international public* (1955), p. 66.

23. See for example, R.Y. Jennings, The progress of international law, *34 B.Y.I.L.* (1958) p. 334.

24. Codification and development of international law, *49 A.J.I.L.* (1955) p. 16.

25. *Op. cit.* at p. 17.

similar *lacunae* in well-developed systems of municipal law. In 1844, an eminent British judge could say of what was, even at that date, the fairly well-developed English legal system:

> "If a statistical table of legal propositions should be drawn out, and the first column headed "Law by Statute", and the second "Law by Decision", a third column, under the heading "Law taken for granted" would comprise as much matter as both the others combined".[26]

Lauterpacht then proceeds to distinguish two classes of situation in which there is divergence of practice and lack of agreement as to the applicable law: the first being that in which the reasons for the lack of agreement are not related to the interests of States, and therefore are "intrinsically of little moment",[27] and the other where the lack of agreement is "due to conflicting interests and claims in the political, economic and strategic spheres".[28] Codification is just as desirable, the learned author argues, in each of these two situations, but the actual work necessary to bring it about is different: in one case, the aim must be

> "to bring about uniformity by persuasion and instruction",

and in the other

> "to bring about an agreed rule of law . . . where no less persuasion and instruction, coupled with . . . a practical and statesmanlike reconciliation of opposing principles and considerations, are required as a condition of the emergence of an agreed rule".[29]

However, the learned author somewhat destroys the force of his own case with regard to the first type of situation, by conceding that so far as the example he chooses to illustrate it is concerned, namely the question of whether ratification of a treaty is required for it to come into force, if the treaty itself is silent on the point,

> "the importance of the subject appears in the proper perspective if it is recalled that practically all treaties regulate the matter one way or the other".[30]

The first point to be observed is therefore that there is such a thing, in the field of international law, as "lawyers' law", vexed questions which it is unnecessary to resolve by codification (or

26. *O'Connell* v. *Regina*, (1844) 11 Cl. & F., p. 155 at p. 372, per Lord Denman.
27. *Op. cit.*, p. 23.
28. *Op. cit.*, p. 24.
29. *Op. cit.*, p. 27.
30. *Op. cit.*, p. 24; [cf. Vienna Convention on the Law of Treaties arts. 12 and 14 and art. 24, paragraph 1; see Briggs in *126 Recueil des Cours*, 1969-I, at pp. 244-256.]

otherwise) because the uncertainties and gaps which fall into this category, however much academic controversy they may provoke, do not give rise to problems in practice, in the relationships between States. A gap or uncertainty in customary law is not unlikely, in the nature of things, to result from the fact that the point in question has never mattered enough to States to have been the subject of any claims or challenges, which would have generated practice to settle the matter one way or the other.

The second observation which is appropriate here is that the underlying philosophy of codification, for many of its adherents, may be thought to be expressed in Lauterpacht's statement that

> "the absence of an agreed rule is a greater evil than the adoption of a rule which is perhaps not as good as the one which could have been adopted".[31]

This observation is made with reference to the first category of situations distinguished by Lauterpacht, namely that in which the lack or uncertainty of the law does not result from the clash of State interests, but it does seem also to have governed his thinking as to the merits of codification in areas of political delicacy also. Whether the principle is really as self-evident as it would appear is certainly open to question: but Lauterpacht does in any event go on to approve, somewhat inconsistently, the possibility of interfering with a generally accepted rule of law in the name of considerations of "progress, of mutuality of enlightened economic interest, of international interdependence, of good faith, of morality, of the rights of man";[32] this in connection with the work of the International Law Commission on the question of statelessness.

The true justification for the Law Commission's intereference in this field, which as Lauterpacht laments, did not meet with such a favourable reception from States as it might have been expected to deserve, was that it was asked to take such action by the Economic and Social Council,[33] and such an invitation might have been taken to show that States themselves, or a reasonable number of them, desired some development in this branch of the law. The sequel shows that this was not the case, or alternatively that the

31. *Op. cit.*, p. 24.
32. *Op. cit.*, p. 29.
33. See Resolution 319.B.III (XI) of the Economic and Social Council, 11 August 1950.

precise developments proposed by the International Law Commission were not those desired.

The point which the case of the International Law Commission's work on statelessness illustrates is that although codification may justifiably seek to change the law so far as necessary to make it consistent and orderly and complete, it should not seek to abrogate clear and definite rules in the name of moral considerations, or other considerations of the kind enumerated in the quotation last made above from Lauterpacht's article, unless it is clear that the existing rules are regarded by the generality of States as unsatisfactory. If this can be shown to be the case, then intereference by "codification" may be justified as anticipating the changes which State practice would eventually have made. In the case of statelessness, the comparative paucity of support received by the Convention opened for signature on 30 August 1961 suggests that in this field codification in the sense of alteration may have been premature.

The would-be codifier of international customary law should bear in mind that such law has something in common with a set of steppingstones laid in the bed of a stream. Provided the stones are sufficient in number and appropriately placed for it to be possible to get across dry-shod (i.e. the usual or frequent practical problems of inter-State relations can be solved), the gaps between the stones are of little importance. Codification involves the building of a bridge, which is only necessary if the stones are inadequate; and – to maintain the metaphor – if the bridge-builders disturb the stepping-stones without themselves achieving a solid structure of their own, the last state will be worse than the first.

It will be clear from what has been said as to the techniques of codification that the expression "the codification of international law" must not be allowed to mislead: codification up to the present time has proceeded on the basis of introducing new law only on the basis of one of the existing sources of law, and a "code" in the field of international law has no intrinsic value of its own. In municipal legal systems, a "code" is an act of the legislature, and derives its force as law from that fact; there is therefore no more difficulty in ascertaining the formal source of the law in such a case than there is with regard to any other piece of municipal legislative activity.

In international relations, on the other hand, it has only been possible to speak of "international legislation" in a sense so different from the meaning of the term in municipal law as to make it essentially a term of art in its own right, to which no argument of analogy from municipal law should properly be applied.[34] The question whether, through and as a result of the existence of the international organisations of the present day, true legislative acts in the international sphere are now possible is a difficult one, which is examined separately below.

Thus the codification of international law has meant only, in the words of Basdevant,

> "un moyen technique pour contribuer à l'efficacité du droit international en ajoutant, par la forme écrite, et d'ordinaire par la forme conventionnelle, plus de précision et de certitude aux règles de ce droit".[35]

A code of international law is not itself a formal source of law by virtue of being a code; it derives its force from the fact that it either expresses in convenient and sytematic form existing rules of general international law, or is contained in a treaty, and has therefore the force of *droit conventionnel* as between the parties to the treaty. A code which has neither the form of a treaty nor the force of existing customary law may of course be taken up into subsequent State practice so as to express, *ex post facto*, as it were, general rules of law,[36] but in such a case the code clearly remains no more than a material source of law.

It should not be overlooked, when speaking of codification by law-making treaty, that not merely has the distinction between "law-making" and other treaties been attacked, but it has also been powerfully argued[37] that no treaty is a source of law in the strict sense, but that treaties are only a source of obligation; that law is something which applies generally, of its own force, to all members of the relevant community or legal order, and not merely

34. The term was used by Manley Hudson for his monumental collection of "law-making" treaties, on the ground that it "would seem to describe quite usefully both the process and the product of the conscious effort to make additions to, or changes in, the law of nations. While it is a term of some apparent novelty, it has come into such common use that it may now [Hudson was writing in 1931] be employed with little hesitation" *International Legislation*, Vol. I, Introduction, p. xiii.

35. *Annuaire de l'Institut*, 1947, p. 227.

36. On this process with regard to a treaty-instrument, see *North Sea Continental Shelf* cases, *I.C.J. Reports 1969*, p. 3, at p. 41, para. 71,

37. By Sir Gerald Fitzmaurice in *Symbolae Verzijl* (1958) pp. 153ff.; see also *92 Recueil des Cours*, 1957-II, p. 97.

to those who have become parties to some instrument. Neither the generality of the principle laid down in the treaty, not the degree of generality of accession to the treaty, according to this view, affects the matter; if the rules laid down are not already rules of law,

> "the parties apply the treaty, not as law, but as an obligation *inter se* which antecedent general law respecting treaties compels them to carry out because they have undertaken to do so . . . the technical position would not really be any different even if it should happen that all the States of the world became parties to a treaty, and it were *soi-disant* "law-making" in character . . . the basis of the obligation is and remains conventional, not statutory".[38]

Professor Jennings regards this thesis as

> "one of those axioms that may remain undiscovered for generations; but once it has been stated is so obviously true as to compel acceptance";[39]

but while the logic of the distinction between source of law and source of obligation (for a full exposition of which reference should be made to Sir Gerald Fitzmaurice's paper) is certainly compelling, some doubt may be felt about the actual usefulness of the distinction in any discussion of the effects of treaties, particularly those which are "*soi-disant* 'law-making' in character".

On the basis of Sir Gerald Fitzmaurice's distinction, a "code" of international law produced in the form of a multilateral treaty is, except insofar as it represents or becomes customary law, a code of obligations accepted by the States parties to the treaty, but not law. If the field covered by the treaty were one which was more or less unregulated by custom, and regulated in detail by the treaty, the consequence would be that in that field the only "law" between the parties would be the single rule "*pacta sunt servanda*". While this conclusion is logically correct if the linguistic distinction (for it is suggested that it is really only a distinction of nomenclature) between sources of law and sources of obligation is accepted, it would surely not correspond to the terminological usage of the States concerned, and their advisers, who would regard the obligations contained in the treaty as "the law" of the Congo basin, or the continental shelf, or outer space, or whatever the field covered by the treaty might be.

In short, it is suggested that with regard particularly to "law-

38. Fitzmaurice, *op. cit.*, pp. 159-160.

39. Recent Developments in the International Law Commission: its Relation to the Sources of International Law, *I.C.L.Q.*, 1964, p. 385 at p. 388.

making" treaties, the distinction between sources of law and sources of obligation is not useful, and tends to create confusion.[40] Obligations imposed by a treaty are legal obligations; they are clearly not obligations on the same "level" as the rule *pacta sunt servanda*, since it is from that rule that they derive their force, but whether one says that they are "law" or "legal obligations" or (as does the Code civil) that they

> "tiennent lieu de loi à ceux qui les [*sc.* les conventions] ont faites",[41]

is a question of linguistic convenience. It would be equally possible to argue that custom is a source of obligation, and not of law; and that the only "law" in the field is the rule that rules which are accepted by State practice accompanied by *opinio juris* are binding on States, i.e. a rule that *consuetudo est servanda.*[42] If, on the other hand, customary rules are rules "of law" and treaty rules are not, the effect of a treaty which waives a right or obligation deriving from custom is that "law" can be set aside and replaced by something which is not "law", which is perhaps curious.[43]

We shall therefore continue unrepentantly to speak of treaties as sources of law, and codified law as deriving from multilateral treaties, since this appears to be the most convenient terminology, and corresponds to what the parties to a codifying treaty believe that they are doing. We shall however generally avoid the term "law-making treaties", in view of its unpopularity, and in view of the implication it appears to carry that certain treaties make law, and others merely create legal obligations. We can certainly agree with Sir Gerald Fitzmaurice (and others) that whatever it is that treaties create – law or legal obligations – all treaties must have the same basic effects.

Reference will therefore normally be made in this study to "codifying treaties" or "codifying conventions". It will have

40. In this sense, cf. Sørensen in *101 Recueil des Cours,* 1960-III, at p. 53.

41. Code civil, art. 1134.

42. [This is in fact the view of the modern Italian school:] Cf. Sereni, *Diritto internazionale, Vol. I, p. 116;* [Quadri, *Droit international public, 113 Recueil des Cours,* 1964-III, p. 245 at p. 321; Morelli, *Nozioni di diritto internationale, p. 25.*]

43. This is of course the whole distinction between *jus cogens* and *jus dispositivum*; but it is because very nearly all of international law falls into the latter category that in the present writer's view it is essential to regard obligations deriving from treaty as equally a form of *jus*.

become clear from the discussion of the concept of codification given above that there does not seem to us to be much point in trying to distinguish between codification as re-statement of existing law and codification as involving at least some degree of "progressive development". Most treaties, if not all, will contain both elements in some degree and in varying proportions. It may sometimes be convenient to distinguish between instruments which are codifying *stricto sensu*, that is to say instruments which, or the provisions whereof under study which, are limited to a re-statement in treaty form of rules which already exist (plus or minus a few nuances) as part of general international law; and instruments which are only codifying *lato sensu*, that is to say those in which there is a very considerable admixture of new law, based upon but going substantially beyond existing law.

One other distinction which will sometimes prove necessary in practice may be mentioned here, since it will prove to be of considerable importance when we come to consider the position of States which do not accept the rules laid down in a codifying convention, and in particular those States which attach reservations to their ratifications of the convention.

Principles and rules of law may be divided for this purpose into two classes. On the one hand there are rules which govern the relationships between the subjects of international law, rules as to what conduct by a State is – in the widest sense – lawful and what conduct is unlawful, and detailed rules for the precise implementation of the obligations of a State or other subject of international law. On the other hand there are principles and rules which are not so much related to conduct as to concepts: the concept "State" carries with it certain legal consequences, and the concept "international tort" carries with it "duty to make reparation",[44] for example. Most of the rules in this latter class have as their distinguishing mark that it is not possible for any agreement between States to set them aside. Thus if a State acts contrary to some essential aspect of its Statehood, if for example it parts with all its territory, irrevocably and definitively, it cannot, by agreement with its one-time neighbours, continue to be a State; and while the right to reparation for an international wrong may be waived, it is not possible to agree that an international wrong is

44. See *Chorzow Factory (Jurisdiction), P.C.I.J. Series A, No. 9*, p. 21.

not, or shall not be, an international wrong, without losing touch altogether with the concept.

This distinction is not identical with the distinction between *jus dispositivum* and *jus cogens*: the concept of *jus cogens* is roughly the equivalent on the international plane of *ordre public*, whereas what we are discussing is not whether it is in the interests of the international community that States should be permitted to agree to a certain end, but what are the concepts of international law which exist so undeniably that States cannot agree to ignore them. The dividing line is narrow between agreeing to waive or vary rules which flow from a certain concept, and denying the concept, but it does exist and must sometimes be drawn.

A codifying convention may thus lay down rules of conduct, which States may abide by or may agree between themselves to waive, generally or otherwise. Such a convention may however also declare the existence of a concept of international law which, if it is or becomes a generally recognised part of the law, cannot be wholly ignored or denied. Thus, as we shall see, even if it were general law that the delimitation of the continental shelf should be effected between adjacent States by application of the "equidistance method", which the International Court has ruled is not the case, it would remain possible for States to agree on some other methods: but no State which has a continental shelf can rid itself of it, except by actual transfer of its rights, and no land-locked State can claim a continental shelf, because – whatever degree of agreement such claims might encounter, short of universal acceptance resulting in a change in the law – such claims are totally inconsistent with the concept of the continental shelf, and therefore with international law itself.

[This distinction between principles and rules which express basic concepts on the one hand, and principles and rules relating to conduct on the other, necessitates one further clarification. It is not here asserted that the principles and rules of the former class derive their particular status from their embodying some sort of "natural law", or from their resulting by necessity from the organization of the international community. The "concepts" which we are dealing with contain within themselves a whole series of ideas which can be expressed as principles or rules affecting the conduct of States; but that is not to say either that the concepts could not have been other than they are, or that all the rules they enshrine necessarily follow from the concepts, as pure concepts. The concept "State" in positive international law entails *(inter alia)* the possession of a defined territory; but there is nothing in logic or nature which would have forbidden international law to have developed a concept of a "State" which did not invariably fulfil the condition of territory – if, for example, historical developments had rendered it necessary or desirable for the example of the Order of Malta to be widely imitated. As things are, it is nonetheless not possible for a State to part irrevocably with the whole of its territory and yet remain a State.

In short, derogations from principles of the class we are considering are not permitted, not because they are matters of *jus cogens*, nor because they enshrine some sort of *jus naturale*, but because they are such that derogation from them implies a denial that they are *jus*, with consequences for the whole international community.]

Chapter Three

THE SOURCES OF LAW IN THE MODERN INTERNATIONAL COMMUNITY

As we have noted, one of the most marked results of the far-reaching changes in the political shape of the world and in the legal relationships of States to be observed today has been a marked shift in emphasis as between the various recognised sources of international law. While the majority of text-books continue to lay down the perfectly correct statement that the two principal sources of international law are custom and treaties,[1] along with the "general principles of law" and the subsidiary sources mentioned in Article 38 (1) (d) of the Statute of the International Court of Justice, the practical day-to-day importance of treaties, particularly of multilateral treaties, increases steadily at the expense of that of international customary law. [Even where the matter in question is one regulated by customary law and not (as between the relevant States) by treaty, if there is a multilateral treaty in the field it will tend to be invoked in support of the customary rule. Thus in the recent case concerning the *Legal Consequences for States of the Continued Presence of South Africa in Namibia,* the International Court quoted from Article 60 of the Vienna Convention on the Law of Treaties – which is of course not yet in force – to support its argument on the question of termination of treaties, observing that

> "The rules laid down by the Vienna Convention . . . may in many respects be considered as a codification of existing customary law on the subject".[2]]

Furthermore, from various quarters claims are made that a new source of law, entitled to the description of "international legisla-

1. See, for example: Oppenheim (8th ed. by Lauterpacht), Vol. I, p. 25; Schwarzenberger, *Manual of International Law,* p. 28; Cavaré, *Le droit international public positif,* Vol. I, p. 214; Balladore-Pallieri, *Diritto internazionale publico,* pp. 74 and 80; Accioly, *Tratado de direito internacional público,* p. 33; Moreno Quintana, *Tratado de derecho internacional,* Vol. I, p. 70; Verdross, *Völkerrecht,* p. 137ff.

2. [*I.C.J. Reports 1971,* at. p. 47, para. 94.]

tion" has come into being, although most of its exponents are ready to admit that it does not, or does not yet, have all the qualities and attributes of legislation as that term is understood in municipal law.[3]

Throughout at least the greater part of its history, international law has lacked any sort of legislative organ; the nearest approach to such a thing prior to the developments following the creation of the United Nations Organization was probably the law-making activities of the Concert of Europe, which – however contrary to the modern egalitarian concepts of sovereignty of States it may have been – did in fact operate to create general law on the international plane. But on the whole, for international law what in many municipal systems, particularly codified systems, was the exception had perforce to become the rule: as Portalis expressed it

> "une foule de choses sont nécessairement abandonnées à l'empire de l'usage, à la discussion des hommes instruits, à l'arbitrage des juges".[4]

We have here in a nutshell, if not a precise enumeration of the sources of law, in the strict sense of formal sources, at least a convenient summary of the methods, other than legislative, by which the law may grow and develop to keep pace with the changing needs of the community. These are, then: custom; the influence of legal writing (doctrine); and judicial settlement and judicial precedent.

An overall view of the development of international law through the years will show that each of these elements of legal development has had its season of ascendancy, and that there has been a continual shifting of the balance between them; but none has ever ceased entirely to exert its influence, and until the present day at least, no radically new factor has become added to those mentioned.

That what Portalis calls "la discussion des hommes instruits" has still some role to play is undeniable if, for example, one examines the Reports of the Judgments and Advisory opinions of the International Court of Justice, and of its predecessor, the Permanent Court of International Justice. Article 38 (1) (d) of the Court's Statute expressly directs the Court to apply, "as subsidiary

3. See for example O'Connell, *International Law,* Vol. I, p. 4.

4. Discours préliminaire; Fenet, *Recueil complet des travaux préparatoires du Code civil,* Vol. I, p. 467.

means for the determination of rules of law", "the teachings of the most highly qualified publicists", and although the Court itself, with a very proper judicial remoteness, refrains from quoting or referring directly to legal authors, however eminent,[5] the separate and dissenting opinions of the individual Members of the Court draw liberally on the views of jurists.[6] It is also arguable, to say the least, that it is through the writings of legal authors that the "general principles of law" mentioned in Article 38 (1) (c) of the Statute acquire form and shape, so as to become suitable for adoption as the grounds of a decision.[7] Nevertheless, it is highly inlikely that any modern jurist will ever be able to exert such an influence on his own or subsequent ages as did the "founding fathers" of international law, so as to be cited in the same breath as Grotius, Vattel, Bynkershoek, Pufendorf and Suarez. The age of *doctrine* is past, perhaps never to return.[8]

As to settlement of the law by judicial decision, and the creation of judicial precedents – also classed by Article 38 (1) (d) as a subsidiary source – it must be admitted that the development of international law by this means is a very recent phenomenon, usually dated from, at the earliest, the Jay Treaty between Great Britain and the U.S.A. It must not be overlooked that, as Professor Friedmann has observed,

> "If it is the principal purpose of law to substitute the peaceful settlement of disputes, and of other relations between groups and individuals, for the use of force, international law did not until the League of Nations Covenant of 1919 even aspire to such a function".[9]

Law does not develop of its own motion, but only as development is required by the development of relationships in the society in

5. See Lauterpacht, *The Development of International Law by the International Court,* p. 23.

6. See, for example, the Joint Dissenting Opinion of Judges Guerrero, McNair, Read and Hsu Mo in the *Genocide* case, *I.C.J. Reports 1951,* p. 31, at pp. 32-8, quoting Fauchille, Malkin, Accioly and Podesta Costa.

7. [Cf. also Spiropoulos, *Théorie générale du droit international* (1930) on the role of "l'opinion dominante" in the formation and ascertainment of international law (*op. cit.,* at pp. 17ff.).]

8. Cf. [In this sense, Wolfke, *Custom in Present International Law,* pp. 151-152; see] however Cavaré, *Le droit international public positif,* p. 217, for "l'assentiment des gens qui réfléchissent" as an element in the formation of customary law. See also Oppenheim-Lauterpacht, p. 33.

9. *127 Recueil des Cours,* 1969-II, p. 48. Cf. Machiavelli: "Dovete sapere come sono dua generazioni di combattere: l'uno con le leggi, l'altro con la forza" (*Il Principe,* cap. XVIII).

which it operates. The notorious incompleteness of customary law is of less importance in a world in which ultimately solutions to differences are likely to be imposed by the stronger party than in one in which it will be the task of a judge or arbitrator to apply legal principles so far as he can ascertain them.[10]

Thus the movement towards third-party judicial settlement on a basis of law which may be said to have begun with the 1794 Jay Treaty, and to have culminated in the establishment of the Permanent Court of International Justice, both created a need for more precision in international law, and operated – to a limited extent – to satisfy it. Similarly, the decline in both judicial and arbitral settlement of international disputes which is observable today[11] contributes to the very uncertainty of the law which is sometimes advanced as a reason for reluctance to refer disputes to an international tribunal.[12] The process is something of a vicious circle: the only way in which disputed points of law can be resolved in the modern international society in which gunboat diplomacy is frowned upon, assuming that any attempt to agree upon a solution is likely to produce merely a compromise unsatisfactory to both sides, is by reference to a tribunal, preferably the International Court Court of Justice; but States are understandably reluctant to submit their differences to a court if they do not have at least some idea, if not of the result, at least of the factors which will be weighed up to arrive at the result.[13] The eminent American jurist Oliver Wendell Holmes observed in 1897 that

> "the prophecies of what the courts will do in fact, and nothing more pretentious, are what I mean by the law";[14]

and if it is not possible to make such prophecies with any confidence in a given branch of law, one may be forgiven for saying that effectively there is no law on the point; and if there is no law,

10. The present writer does not wish to take sides in the controversy as to the formal completeness of international law, and the role (if any) of *non liquet* in international judicial tribunals. See Lauterpacht in *Symbolae Verzijl* pp. 196ff., and Stone, *Non Liquet* and the Function of Law in the International Community, *35 B.Y.I.L.* (1959), p. 124.

11. See the Report of the Secretary-General of the United Nations, September 1970, paragraphs 144 et seqq.

12. Cf. Briggs in *126 Recueil des Cours,* 1969-I, pp. 299-300.

13. Cf. Jennings, The Progress of International Law, *34 B.Y.I.L.* (1958) at p. 346.

14. O.W. Holmes, *The Path of the Law,* quoted in C.K. Allen, *Law in the Making*, p. 42.

there is little ground for referring the matter to a tribunal to be settled according to law. Explanations of the role of Article 38 (1) (c) of the Statute of the International Court are likely to fall on deaf ears in such a situation.[15]

There remains custom as a source of law, placed by Article 38 of the I.C.J. Statute and by most authors more or less on a level with treaties; however, for the historical perspective we are for the moment adopting, custom may be said to comprehend treaty-law; for it is probably true to say that at least until the nineteenth century, the only influence of treaties on *general* international law – as opposed to the creation of *lex specialis* between the parties – was to the extent that the conclusion of a treaty consistent with the practice of other States might itself be an act of State practice contributing to the formation of custom.

It is customary to date the growth of the modern "law-making" treaty from the Treaty of Vienna, although that Treaty cannot be said to be typical of the more modern brand of multilateral instrument designed to regulate the general legal relationships of the parties – and ultimately of all members of the international community – in a particular field of their activities. This is a trend which has contributed not a little to the present predominance of the treaty as an instrument for development of the law, and to the movement towards codification. As Verdross has put it, codification has pushed customary law somewhat into the background.[16] Nevertheless, it is reasonable to assume that the movement towards an international *lex scripta* which we have been discussing is no more than an example, though a marked one, of the shifts in balance between the various sources of international law which have already occurred in the course of the law's development. It would be unwise, in the light of history, to assume or claim that we are witnessing, or are likely to witness in the near future, any sort of total eclipse of custom as a source of law, as a result of the encroachment of the law-making treaty. The presumption must

15. Cf. MacGibbon in *33 B.Y.I.L.* (1957), p. 135, on the difficulty of promoting compulsory judicial settlement if the law is applied too flexibly so as "to reduce to insignificance the psychologically desirable factor of predictability – especially in a system as centrifugal as international law at its present stage of development".

16. *Völkerrecht,* p. 137; he continues, however: "Es ist aber noch immer von grosser Bedeutung, da keineswegs alle Normen des Völkerrechts kodifiziert sind und da ausserdem in allen Fällen, in denen die Kodifikationen keine neuen Bestimmungen enthalten, auf das VGR zurückgegriffen werden müss."

also, it is suggested, be against the appearance of any wholly new source of law (such as international legislation – an important concept in the light of the growth of international organizations, to be examined below), wholly independent of the traditional sources.

A question which should be asked in this context is whether it is in fact possible for the sources of law in any given community to alter, or whether the rule which lays down what are the sources to be tapped is as unalterable as the proverbial enactments of the Medes and Persians. Is the enumeration of sources in the international community, or to speak more generally, in any community, the description of a closed class; and if not, is it a class which determines its own content, or one of which the content is determined by some rule lying outside the class?

These are questions which require study because they are fundamental to an examination of the relationship *inter se* of the sources of law, such as custom and "code", and to an even greater extent, to any assessment of claims that a new source of law has come into existence.

The doctrine of the sources of international law, in the words of Professor Alf Ross,

> "can never in principle rest on precepts contained in one among the legal sources the existence of which the doctrine itself was meant to prove. The basis of the doctrine of legal sources is in all cases actual practice and that alone".[17]

In other words, treaties are binding in law, and rules established by usage coupled with *opinio juris* are rules of law, simply because the international community is built upon the postulate, or the hypothesis, that this is the case, and not because any rule *of international law* provides that this is the case. Thus the enumeration of the sources of law which is to be found, though not *eo nomine*, in Article 38 of the Statute of the International Court of Justice is not itself a statement of international law, nor, as Lauterpacht called it, a "codification" of an aspect of international law;[18] it is a statement of the *extra-legal* postulates upon which international law stands, or, in Sereni's expression, one of the "principi costituzionali" of international law.[19]

17. Ross, *A textbook of international law* (1947), p. 83, quoted by Fitzmaurice in *Symbolae Verzijl* (1958) p. 161. (The words "in principle" have fallen out in the quotation in *Symbolae Verzijl.*)

18. 1947 Memorandum on Codification: *Collected Papers,* Vol. I, p. 472.

19. Sereni, *Diritto internazionale,* Vol. I, pp. 112ff., at p. 116.

The fundamental question underlying the problem of the possibility of change in the sources of law applicable to a given community is thus essentially an aspect of the natural law versus postivism controversy. If the sources of law are enumerated by a postulate lying outside international law, or a set of such postulates, are those postulates dictated by necessity, are they in fact self-evident, so that they could not be other than they are; or do they result solely, in Professor Ross's words, from "actual practice" – do they, as it were, arise out of the behaviour of the members of the community over a period of time? Any postulates which are rules of natural law in the sense that they could not be otherwise, are clearly incapable of change; whereas postulates resulting solely from the activity of the community will be capable of changing, and will change, as the community itself develops.

In the paper, already referred to,[20] contributed to *Symbolae Verzijl,* Sir Gerald Fitzmaurice discusses the problem of the formal sources of international law, and refers in particular to the rule *pacta sunt servanda.* His conclusion on this point requires to be quoted *in extenso*:

> "What is the conclusion? It is that the sources of international law cannot be stated, or cannot fully or certainly be stated, in terms of international law itself, and that there are and must be rules of law that have an inherent and necessary validity, in whose absence no system of law at all can exist or be originated. Such a rule, for instance, is the rule *pacta sunt servanda.* This rule does not require to be accounted for in terms of any other rule. It could neither not be, nor be other than what it is. It is not dependent on consent, for it would exist without it. There *could* not be a rule that *pacta sunt non-servanda,* or *non sunt servanda,* for then the *pacta* would no longer be *pacta.* Nor could there be a rule that *pacta sunt interdum servanda et interdum non sunt servanda.* The idea of *servanda* is inherent and necessary in the term *pacta.*[21]

and he adds a footnote:

> "A logician or modern linguistic analyst would no doubt point out that this is equivalent to saying *pacta sunt pacta.* This is very true, but merely means that basically the proposition *pacta sunt servanda* is a tautology in the same sense that most mathematical propositions are tautologies – the two sides of the equation are merely re-statements or re-arrangements of one another's term. But it is precisely in the tautology that the necessity resides; again as with mathematical propositions which, if correct at all (2+2=4), cannot be other than what they are."[22]

The argument is extremely lucid and compelling, but the present

20. Some problems regarding the formal sources of international law; p. 153.
21. *Op. cit.*, p. 164.
22. *Ibid.,* footnote 1.

writer finds it difficult to accept it as logically inexorable, for the following reason. It must be conceded that mathematical statements of the kind exemplified by 2 + 2 = 4 are tautologous in the sense indicated by Sir Gerald Fitzmaurice, but they are nonetheless useful, inasmuch as they record, in a convenient and simple form, certain facts which can be verified by reference to physical objects. But the usefulness of the statement 2 + 2 = 4 (and for that matter its accuracy) derives solely from the meaning attributed to the symbol "2" and the symbol "4"; if we use the symbol "2" to indicate the number we call "three", and the symbol "4" to indicate the number we call "five", then the statement "2 + 2 = 4" is false, and therefore useless. The reason why the statement is useful in arithmetic, is because the meanings attributed to the symbols *by the science of arithmetic* are such that the statement expresses an *arithmetical* truth.

Similarly, the statement *pacta sunt servanda* derives its meaning and its value from the definitions given to the word "*pacta*" and to the word "*servanda*"; but these definitions are given solely by reference to the science of international law. *Pacta* means certain instruments expressing the will or wills of two more States, satisfying conditions of form and essential validity laid down by international law, and intended to be binding under international law; *servanda* means required by international law to be observed in good faith subject to conditions laid down by international law (e.g., subject to the *rebus sic stantibus* doctrine). Thus the rule *pacta sunt servanda*, if it is to have any useful meaning, must refer to concepts of international law; that is to say, it cannot stand outside international law, as a necessary postulate of inherent validity independently of international law.

Even when expressed in the most simple and self-contained form, the statement that, e.g., "acts intended by States to be binding, are binding" is not self-evident or necessary; the law may impose conditions, such as the requirement of consideration in the English law of contracts, without which there is no duty (to observe an agreement) which is imposed by the law, whatever the intentions, or the moral commitments, of the parties may be. The only inherently necessary statement which can be made in this field is that agreements regarded *by the law* as binding (*pacta*) are binding *in law (servanda*), which is not in any sense a postulate underlying international law (or any other system), but a pure tautology which, unlike the statement $2 + 2 = 4$, is of no intrinsic value.

This venture into legal philosophy is necessary merely to dispose of the difficulty in supposing that there could be any alteration in the sources of law if they were, wholly or partially, defined by postulates of intrinsic and necessary validity. It is submitted that although it is true to say that the enumeration of the sources of international law is not itself a rule of international law, it must at the same time be expressed in terms of international law; that although "the law is in the last analysis binding simply because it is the law",[23] this does not mean that the sources of law are the sources, and the only sources, simply because that is the necessary consequence of the existence of the law. The enumeration of the source of the law is, as it were, a function of the development of the community; and there is no obstacle of theory to the alteration of that enumeration resulting, as did the original enumeration, from the requirements of the community. As a community develops, the sources of law which it recognises may change, not merely in relative importance (the process we have already examined) but in effective existence: new sources may be tapped, and old ones cease to flow.

Thus while it is not logically excluded that an additional source of law may come to exist, and generate rules binding on the whole, or possibly some part only, of the international community, this obviously cannot be expected to be a common phenomenon. Furthermore, it is submitted that there is a vital qualification to be made to the statement that new sources may come to exist: it is not possible for a rule to the effect that such-and-such a new source of law exists to enter the international legal order otherwise than through an existing source of law recognised by the international community. [This follows from the nature of the idea of "sources": the rule or postulate which lays down what the sources of law are in a given community must be, at a given moment, an exhaustive statement of the ways in which law can be made and by which law can be changed; it is what Professor Hart[24] has called a "secondary" principle, and its purpose is to ensure stability and certainty in the ascertainment of law. If however it is contended that a new secondary principle can

23. Sir Gerald Fitzmaurice, in *92 Recueil des Cours,* 1957-II, p. 46.
24. H.L.A. Hart, *The Concept of Law,* Oxford, 1961, p. 92 ff.

come into existence, laying down that law may be made – and the existing law thereby changed – by a means not provided for in the existing secondary principle, and that the new secondary principle also itself may come into existence by a means not provided for in the existing secondary principle, then either the new secondary principle is postulating its own existence, so that the argument is a *petitio principii,* or the existing secondary principle is not exhaustive, which we have postulated that it is.

It is therefore clear that new sources of law can only come into existence other than through the operation of an existing source if the secondary principle which enumerates the sources of law is treated from the outset as non-exhaustive; in other words, if the whole concept of sources as a closed class is jettisoned. It may therefore be useful to examine briefly two modern theories of international law which do just that.

It has been claimed by Professor Quadri that he was the first to eliminate the notion of sources from the general system of international law.[25] He conceives of international law as founded on the will of the community, as distinct from the will of States considered *ut singuli,* and distinguishes two classes of norms imposed by the authority of the community on the States which compose it: the first is that of primary norms, which are produced directly by the community-will; one of these primary norms may be, and in the existing international legal order is, a norm laying down procedures by which other norms may be created, the norms so produced being secondary norms. The concept of a "source" is treated by Quadri as wholly inapplicable to the primary norms, which constitute a purely psychological phenomenon; like Topsy, they just "growed".[26] Thus not merely can the norm which lays down the methods of production of secondary norms change spontaneously, but new primary norms – which are directly applicable as law just as much as the secondary norms are – may come into existence spontaneously.[27] In Professor Quadri's construction of the international legal order, new sources

25. *Diritto internazionale pubblico,* (1968) p. 107.

26. H. Beecher Stowe, *Uncle Tom's Cabin,* chap. 20.

27. *Diritto internazionale pubblico,* pp. 25ff., 106ff.; Droit international public, *113 Recueil des cours,* 1964-III, 237, at pp. 319ff. Professor Ago adopts a similar view, but whereas for Quadri customary law rules are secondary norms, for Ago they are part of the *jus non scriptum* formed by the body of primary norms: see Science juridique et droit international, *90 Receuil des cours,* 1956-II, p. 851.

of law may easily come into existence without their creation being the effect of the operation of an existing source.

A more recent theory is that of Professor d'Amato, who dismisses the terms "sources" and "evidences" of international law as "best relegated to the domain of counter-productive terminology",[28] and in effect rejects the concepts of sources and evidences also inasmuch as they "create more problems and ambiguities than they can possibly solve".[29] The place of a theory of sources in Professor d'Amato's system is in effect taken first by the concept of consensus as not merely producing international law, but actually being itself international law,[30] and secondly by a division of norms into primary and secondary legal rules, avowedly on the lines adopted by Professor Hart.[31] The notion of consensus has been most fully worked out by Professor d'Amato in connection with the legal effects of resolutions of the General Assembly of the United Nations, and it will be more convenient to examine it in that context,[32] merely noting here that although he is at pains to emphasise that consensus is law, not a source of law, he does in fact treat it in his book on the concept of customary law as something which in traditional terminology would be called a source.[33]

With regard to the division of rules into primary and secondary, unfortunately Professor d'Amato permits himself a slight looseness of terminology which makes it difficult to summarise his argument. In effect, he distinguishes three classes of rules: (a) rules which are the direct product of international consensus, and which indicate to States what they must or must not do; (b) rules which are similarly the product of international consensus, and which specify the ways in which rules indicating to States what they must or must not do may be created, ascertained, or changed; and (c) rules which derive from the methods of creation or ascertainment of rules laid down in class (b), and which indicate to States what they must or must not do. For these three classes, Professor

28. *The Concept of Custom in International Law,* p. 268.

29. *Op. cit.,* p. 264.

30. See in particular d'Amato, On Consensus, *Canadian Yearbook of International Law,* 1970, p. 104; and *The Concept of Custom in International Law,* p. 33ff.

31. *The Concept of Law,* pp. 92ff.

32. See below, pp. 76-77.

33. Thus, for example, he refers to rules as "*products* of a clear international consensus"; *op. cit.* at p. 41.

d'Amato only makes the two terms "primary" and "secondary" available, thus leaving it obscure whether the division is that of Hart (primary = laying down what States must or must not do, secondary = indicating the ways in which primary rules may be ascertained, produced, or varied) or that of Quadri (primary = directly derived from – in this case – consensus, secondary = derived from the operation of a primary rule enumerating means of creation of secondary norms). For this reason, the present writer is not entirely confident that he has drawn the correct conclusions from Professor d'Amato's analysis; but it would seem to be right to read him as implying that what consensus has done, consensus can undo and re-do, and that the class of rules indicating how rules of direct application may be altered or added to can itself be altered or added to.

To do justice to the theories of Professor Quadri and Professor d'Amato would not only take us too far afield for the purposes of the present study, but would also require far fuller explanation of their views than the extremely compressed, and inevitably therefore slightly distorted, summaries given above. The point sought to be made here is that the writer finds these views unconvincing, partly for the very reason that they leave wide open the possibility of law creation through sources which are neither already recognised, nor themselves created through the operation of recognised sources. As already observed, the purpose of a theory of sources is to ensure stability and certainty;[34] and for this reason, it appears axiomatic that the class of sources should be a closed class, not in the sense of being invariable, but in the sense we have indicated, namely, of being variable only through a change brought about by the operation of one of the recognised sources, one of the members of the class.

The point can be illustrated, without reference to the question of the existence or usefulness of "international legislation", as follows.] It would be theoretically possible for the Judgments – and even the Advisory opinions – of the International Court of Justice to become recognised as a full formal source of international law in their own right, as it were, and not merely as "subsidiary means for the determination of rules of law", in the words of Article 38 (1) (d) of the Court's Statute, in the sense that they would operate to state the law with binding force for all

34. See Hart, *The Concept of Law*, pp. 89ff.

States parties to the Court's Statute, or even for all members of the international community.[35] But apart from the need first to overcome the clear terms of Article 59 of the Statute,[36] this could only occur in one of two ways: either because in a revised version of the Court's Statute, or in some other international treaty-instrument,[37] it were specifically agreed between the States parties to the instrument that this should be so (thus generating a rule of treaty-law), or if a generally accepted practice grew up of regarding Judgments of the Court as binding on States other than the parties to the cases in which they were given, so as to give rise to a rule of customary international law – or of course by some combination of the two processes.[38]

However desirable such a development might be, it would clearly be contrary to legal logic either to regard the International Court as being, by reason of its inherent nature as a Court, in some position above and outside the framework of international law, so as to be able to impose its Judgments on all States by injecting them, as expressions of new rules of law, into the international legal order, as a legislature can inject a new rule into the general municipal law of a State; or to regard its Judgments as capable of acquiring binding force throughout the international community by their own intrinsic power, so as to pull themselves up by their own boot-straps, so to speak.

The point may seem an obvious one, so expressed; but once again, what must be carefully guarded against is becoming victims of our own terminology, and supposing that a "precedent" is binding because of the municipal rule of *stare decisis,* or that international legislation, whatever that may mean, is binding because it is legislative.

It is possible to contend, as for example does Professor Skubiszewski,[39] that "law made by international organizations" is a fourth "category" of law, alongside custom, treaty-law and general

35. Sir Gerald Fitzmaurice, in the paper already referred to, argues very convincingly that this is already in effect the case to a much larger extent than would appear from a statement of the theoretical position in law: see *Symbolae Verzijl,* p. 153 at pp. 168ff.

36. "The decision of the Court has no binding force except between the parties and in respect of that particular case."

37. The Statute, as an "integral part" of the Charter, is clearly a treaty (Charter, Article 92).

38. See G.I. Tunkin, Coexistence and International Law, *95 Recueil des Cours* 1958-III, at pp. 29-30.

39. Enactment of Law by International Organizations, *41 B.Y.I.L.* (1965-6), p. 198.

principles of law, that is to say, a separate source of law; but it must be possible to show, if this view is to be accepted, that "law made by international organizations" has become such a category or source by virtue either of treaty-law, customary law, or the impact of general principles of law. Nor does Professor Skubiszewski in fact argue otherwise: he contends that the validity, effectiveness, application etc., of law-making decisions of international organizations are

> "governed not by the law of treaties but solely by the law of the international organization which is the author of the act ";[40]

but it is nonetheless the case that the penultimate reason why such acts possess validity at all as law (or as legal obligation)[41] is because the constituent treaty of the organization, possibly in conjunction with subsequent customary law, operates to that effect; and the ultimate reason is the rule *pacta sunt servanda.*

Professor Friedmann apparently takes a more radical view, when he asserts that

> "It has . . . come to be increasingly recognised that, apart from the traditional sources of law-making, custom and treaty, we must look to other sources of international law",[42]

But although he quotes with approval the views of Asamoah on the legal effects of United Nations decisions (to be discussed later),[43] it does not appear from Professor Friedmann's treatment of declaratory resolutions of the General Assembly as a "source" of law that he means any more than that such resolutions may contribute to the development of international law in the way, already discussed, in which any international instrument may assist the crystallisation of law.[44] There can be no doubt that such resolutions do have an important contribution to make to the development of international law in this way, but this does not, as Professor Friedmann recognises, give them a legislative character.

It follows that in discussing the legal effect and nature of such acts as General Assembly resolutions, we must bear in mind that – setting aside the argument that such resolutions may have

40. *41 B.Y.I.L.* (1965-66), p. 198, at p. 221.

41. See the discussion of the views of Sir Gerald Fitzmaurice, above, pp. 26-27.

42. *127 Recueil des Cours,* 1969-II, p. 142.

43. Asamoah, *The Legal Significance of the Declarations of the General Assembly of the United Nations* (The Hague, 1966); see below, pp. 63ff.

44. 127 *Recueil des Cours,* 1969-II, at pp. 143-146.

legal force as authoritative interpretations of the UN Charter[45] – what is called international legislation must derive its force, either mediately or immediately, from treaty-law or from customary international law. It is not simply a question, as has been suggested,[46] of the absence of any mention of this sort of law-making activity from the enumeration of sources in Article 38 of the Statute of the International Court of Justice; if it is accepted, as surely cannot be disputed, that at the time when the Statute was drafted, the enumeration was complete, then any alleged fresh source of law not therein mentioned must at least be able to prove a genealogical link with one or more of the sources which are so mentioned.

45. Asamoah, *The Legal Significance of the Declarations of the General Assembly of the United Nations,* p. 12ff.

46. Asamoah, *op. cit.*, p. 54; see also Skubiszewski, 41 *B.Y.I.L.* (1965-66) p. 198 at p. 244, [and Falk, On the Quasi-Legislative Competence of the General Assembly, 60 *A.J.I.L.* (1966), p. 782.]

Chapter Four

THE NATURE AND THE FORMATION OF INTERNATIONAL CUSTOMARY LAW

A much quoted observation of Basdevant, dating from 1936, is to the effect that

> "les idées des juristes sur le caractère de la coutume n'ont atteint ni à l'unité ni à la clarté".[1]

It is regrettably the fact that between 1936 and the present day unity has still not been achieved, although a certain amount more clearness may be reckoned as the achievement of a number of successive Judgments of the International Court of Justice and of the numerous writers who have tackled the problem.[2] In view of the continuing divergences of opinion on the subject, it will be advisable, before proceeding further with our study of the role of custom in present-day international law, briefly to discuss the significance of the concept of custom, and to touch on some of the controversies surrounding it, in order to show how the view one takes of customary law, and particularly of the way in which it comes into existence, necessarily affects the view taken of the present and future part to be played by custom in developing the law.

The generally held view of customary law, which has been endorsed by the International Court of Justice,[3] is that the creation of a rule of customary international law postulates

> "two constitutive elements: (1) a general practice of States and (2) the acceptance by States of the general practice as law".[4]

1. Règles générales de la paix, *Recueil des Cours* 1936-IV p. 508; quoted (for example) by Kunz, The Nature of Customary International Law, 47 *A.J.I.L.* (1953) p. 663.

2. This is not the place for an extensive bibliography: the two works which the present writer has found most stimulating are Søensen, *Les sources du droit international* (Copenhagen, 1946) and the article by Kunz cited in the previous note.

3. See particular *Continental Shelf* cases, *I.C.J. Reports* 1969, p. 3, at p. 44.

4. Schwarzenberger, *A Manual of International Law*, (1967), p. 32.

In the past, the first of these two elements has not given rise to any serious difficulties of legal theory, however difficult it may be in practice to ascertain or decide whether there exists a general practice of States, and if so, what is its precise content. We shall have occasion to discuss the question of what sort of acts may be taken into account in assessing State practice, in the course of our examination of the modern concept of international legislation;[5] for the moment, the nature of the *opinio juris sive necessitatis* should first be considered.

The precise definition of the *opinio juris*, the psychological element in the formation of custom, the philosophers' stone which transmutes the inert mass of accumulated usage into the gold of binding legal rules, has probably caused more academic controversy than all the actual contested claims made by States on the basis of alleged custom, put together. A present-day writer may be understandably reluctant to call upon his readers to devote further time to this juridical squaring of the circle, but it is impossible to discuss the future of customary law without some study of the elements which are regarded as going to its making.

The simple equation of the *opinio juris* with the intention to conform to what is recognised, at the moment of conforming, as an existing rule of law has been exposed to the objection of Kelsen and others[6] – which, on its own terms, is unanswerable – that it necessarily implies a vicious circle in the logical analysis of the creation of custom. As a usage appears and develops, States may come to consider the practice to be required by law before this is in fact the case; but if the practice cannot become law until States follow it in the *correct* belief that it is required by law, no practice can ever become law, because this is an impossible condition. Nor does the avenue of escape indicated by the tag *communis error facit jus*, i.e., the argument that the belief, even the mistaken belief, of States in the existence of a rule of law requiring them to act, or refrain from acting, in a certain way, is sufficient to create the rule believed in, have many adherents.

The extreme opposite view, the theory that the establishment

5. See below, p. 67.

6. [Mokre, *Theorie des Gewohnheitsrechts*, (1932), p. 166; Kelsen, Théorie du droit international coutumier, *Revue internationale de la Théorie du droit*, 1939, pp. 253ff.; Kunz, The Nature of Customary International Law, 47 A.J.I.L. (1953), p. 662; Quadri, *Diritto internazionale pubblico*, p. 130; and Cours général de droit international public, 113 *Recueil des Cours*, 1964-III, at pp. 323-4.]

of international custom does not require *opinio juris* at all, but that established usage is sufficient without evidence of states of mind, has also comparatively few supporters.[7] [As Professor Zemanek has observed,[8] while the requirement of *opinio juris* does undoubtedly give rise to many problems in practice, particularly with regard to proof of its existence, to assert that it is wholly unnecessary is to "throw out the baby with the bathwater". Furthermore,] it is admittedly difficult to distinguish between usage which has become binding as customary law and usage which has not (apart from cases, such as the *Right of Passage* case before the International Court of Justice,[9] in which the question is largely or entirely one of generality or consistency of practice), without allowing the psychological element in the creation of custom to creep back into the discussion by a devious route and under another name.[10]

A proposal for an interpretation of the traditional concept of the *opinio juris* which would not be subject to the objection that it creates a *circulus inextricabilis* was advanced by Mr. I.C. MacGibbon in 1957.[11] Mr. MacGibbon starts by drawing attention to the importance of distinguishing between customary rules expressed as rights and customary rules expressed as obligations, and argues that the *opinio juris* is principally, if not wholly, of importance from the latter standpoint.

> "It is only with difficulty that it can be conceived that a practice motivated by reasons of convenience or self-interest would have been initiated or evolved under the conviction on the part of the States participating that such a practice was in conformity with law, far less that it was enjoined by law, although such considerations may well apply to the formation of a customary obligation. To hold otherwise would be to suppose that the assertion of a claim, far from being made as of right or in a state of indifference as to whether or not it was in conformity with law, was made as a matter of duty".[12]

7. See for example, Kelsen, Théorie du droit international coutumier, *Révue internationale de la théorie du droit,* 1939, pp. 253ff; Guggenheim, *Lehrbuch des Völkerrechts* (1948), pp. 46-47; Les deux éléments de la coutume en droit international, *Etudes en l'honneur de G.Scelle,* Vol. I, p. 275; [Principes de droit international public, 80 Recueil des Cours, 1952-I, at pp. 70-72.]

8. [Die Bedeutung der Kodifizierung des Völkerrechts für seine Anwendung, in *Festschrift Verdross*, 1971, p. 565 at p. 574.]

9. *Right of Passage over Indian Territory (Merits), I.C.J. Reports 1960,* p.6.

10. [Cf. Tunkin, Remarks on the Juridical Nature of Customary Norms of International Law, 49 *Cal. L.R.* (1961), p. 419 at p. 426, with reference to Guggenheim's paper (*op. cit.,* note 7 above).]

11. Customary International Law and Acquiescence, 33 *B.Y.I.L.*, p. 115.

12. MacGibbon, *op. cit.*, at pp. 127-128.

The distinction is of course a valid one, and it is perfectly correct that a State can hardly be supposed to believe that customary international law requires it to *assert* a certain claim, as opposed to requiring it to admit or recognise the claim of some other State, made in conformity with existing law. But the distinction as expressed by Mr. MacGibbon is in fact an oversimplification of the problem: for the State which asserts a claim will be guided by what it believes to be the law in fixing the *extent* of its claim. The *opinio juris* in the traditional sense does therefore have a real existence and meaning on the side of the State which asserts a right, in that it claims as much and no more as it believes to be due to it,[13] that is to say, it does not *make* its claim because it believes that international law requires it to do so, but it *limits* its claim because it believes that international law requires it to do so.

A further difficulty to which Mr. MacGibbon's thesis gives rise, to be discussed below,[14] is that it virtually excludes from its scope acts of State practice which do not put the States other than that which makes a positive claim or act in a position where they are bound to make their views known: if *opinio juris* normally exists only on the part of the reacting State, and not on the part of the acting States, there can be none where there are no reacting States; and therefore the claim or act in such a case is not relevant in assessing the existence of custom.

[An attempt has recently been made to produce a complete reformulation of the theory of customary law, which would not be subject to the theoretical objections and practical difficulties encountered by the traditionally accepted views; Professor d'Amato, in his recent book,[15] has proposed the abandonment of the concepts of *opinio juris* and usage as the constituent elements of a rule of customary law, and the substitution of "articulation" and an "act or commitment" of a State to take their places.

In Professor d'Amato's proposed system, the qualitative element in the formation of a customary rule, namely "articulation" would differ from the traditional idea of *opinio juris* in that it

13. Of course in practice a State may, and probably will, claim more than it thinks it is entitled to, in the form of a sort of percentage to allow for objections, but this does not affect the point made above.

14. See below, p. 88.

15. *The Concept of Custom in International Law* (Cornell University Press, 1971).

would not be a psychological element in the mind[16] of the State (or States) whose activity is in question, but the objective fact of a written formulation by the State concerned or by some other person or body of a purported "rule of law". Such articulation may be effected by diplomatic correspondence, by a General Assembly resolution, or simply in the writings of a "responsible jurist"; it must also be such as can reasonably be presumed to have come to the notice of the State or States concerned. (We may note that at this point in Professor d'Amato's argument, a "rule of law" presumably denotes a rule which has been advanced as a new rule *de lege ferenda*; for if it were required that a rule must have already been declared to exist, then since *ex hypothesi* we are discussing the stage of the formation of a rule of customary law, the result would be that one would be trapped in the same vicious circle as results from the accepted definition of *opinio juris*.) As for the quantitative element, the "act or commitment" of a State, required in Professor d'Amato's theory to convert the potential, enunciated, rule into an actual rule of customary law, this differs little in essence from the traditional concept of usage, with the vital exception that in Professor d'Amato's construct, a single act or commitment is sufficient to convert the enunciated rule into a rule of customary law.

It is not entirely clear whether the rule so created is considered by Professor d'Amato as a rule which would unquestionably be applied by a tribunal. He asserts, in a hypothetical example of injury by a falling satellite,[17] that an international tribunal would regard such a rule as binding in a parallel case on the basis merely of a single precedent, that is to say if it were shown that on one previous occasion, on a demand by the State of the injured party (the articulation) the State to which the satellite belonged had paid compensation (the act or commitment), even if when so doing it had reserved its legal position. Even if a court were ready automatically to follow such a precedent, it is surely impossible, *pace* Professor d'Amato, that it should do so on the basis of an alleged *customary* rule, in view of the lack of evidence of generality of the practice invoked. In any event, it seems that for Professor d'Amato the question of the probable response of a tribunal to

16. As Professor d'Amato observes, the concept of the "mind" of a State is somewhat artificial; it would however appear to be useful as a sort of shorthand.

17. *Op. cit.*, p. 95.

an alleged rule is not relevant; his theory of customary law is more concerned with the view of the matter taken by the States involved, that is to say, it is, in his expression, "claim-oriented".

The underlying philosophy of this view is expressed as follows:

> "... we must view international law as a psychological bargaining mechanism involving conflicting claims among national decisionmakers and their legal counsel. If we attempt to study international law as it is viewed by participants in the international arena, we will be inclined to replace absolutistic theories with the more accurate description of a *process* by which the better of two conflicting claims prevails. In other words, two competing claimants may each have a case that falls short of fulfilling the requirements for a given absolutistic theory, yet the fact that one claimant has prevailed or will prevail over the other necessitates an abandonment of that 'theory' and its replacement by one which takes account of the *relative* superiority of persuasiveness".[18]

Thus the reason why the elements of generality and repetition have been excluded from Professor d'Amato's conception of the quantitative constituent of a customary rule is because for him a rule of customary law is merely something of a greater or lesser degree of persuasiveness; it is neither a statement of general practice or conformity, nor an assertion of an obligation. Thus both the element of "custom" and the element of "law" in any traditional sense have been whittled down to vanishing point.

As against Professor d'Amato, who cites Heraclitus in support of his approach to international law as an ever-changing process,[19] and who thereby proclaims his allegiance to the school of legal philosophy which we may call *οἱ τὸ πᾶν κινοῦντες*, the present writer unashamedly prefers the more tradition approach of *οἱ τοῦ ὅλου στασιῶται*.[20] (In view of Professor d'Amato's emphasis on the importance of relative persuasiveness, a more tempting distinction is that between the Better and Worse Logics of Aristophanes!)[21] The Heraclitean view of international law does seem to lead to an incomplete view of the nature and genesis of customary international law. The distinguishing character of a *legal* claim, in the sense of a claim that certain conduct is required or justified by law, is surely an implied assertion that an impartial third party, called upon to consider the matter from the stand-

18. *Op. cit.*, p. 18.
19. *Op. cit.*, p. 10.
20. For this distinction, see Plato, Theaetetus, (ed. Heindorf), 181A.
21. "...*ἄμφω τὼ λόγω, τὸν κρείττον', ὅστις ἐστί, καὶ τὸν ἥττονα. τούτοιν τὸν ἕτερον τοῖν λόγοιν, τὸν ἥττονα, νικᾶν λέγοντά φασι τἀδικώτερα.*" (Aristophanes, The Clouds, lines 112-115).

point of law, would decide that the claim was justified. Viewed in this light, persuasiveness does not admit of degrees, since a tribunal or arbitrator must decide either that the claim is justified or that it is not: *tertium non datur.*

Another member of the Heraclitean school, Professor Richard Falk, deprecates any approach to the problem of the sources of international law which is oriented towards law as embodied in the settlement of disputes by the International Court of Justice; he considers that this distorts enquiry

> "by conceiving of law-creation exclusively from the perspective of the rules applicable in this one centralized, judicial institution, an institution that expresses the positivistic assumption that international legal obligations must always be shown to rest upon some tangible evidence of consent on the part of the State that is bound",

and explains that

> "such a perspective overlooks the rôle of unilateral claims to act posited by nation-states and community prescriptions about action laid down by non-judicial international institutions."[22]

But even allowing for Professor Falk's strictures on the judicially-oriented approach,[23] it surely distorts enquiry just as much to concentrate solely on unilateral claims to act – coupled with "articulation" of a legal rule – which might or might not be upheld by a tribunal. Looking at the matter from the point of view of States, of what Professor d'Amato calls national "decision-makers" and their legal advisers, it would seem reasonable to suppose that in a "claim-conflict situation" where both sides could point to "rules of law" in Professor d'Amato's sense, a question which the national decisionmaker would be bound to put to his legal adviser would be: Which view is right? – and this would mean, Which alleged rule represents the correct rule of international law? This in turn means, in the present writer's view, Which rule would be upheld by an impartial tribunal on the basis of international law?

The foregoing analysis of the meaning of the question: Which

22. On the Quasi-legislative Competence of the General Assembly, 60 *A.J.I.L.* (1966) p. 782.

23. Even if Article 38 of the I.C.J. Statute imposes on the Court a positivistic approach, which is not universally accepted, consideration of law from the point of view of an unspecified tribunal need not imply the assumption that consent is the basis of international law.

view is right? , is just as valid if the State in question is not subject to the compulsory jurisdiction of any court, and has no intention of submitting the dispute to any court: any other interpretation makes the question a polititcal or pragmatic one, and not a legal one. While it is true that, in Professor Tammes' words,

> "international law often puts its subjects before a conflict of interests without providing the key to the solution",[24]

this does not mean that a solution does not exist; and it is by the application of "absolutistic" theories – if this means theories which provide a general rule for use in particular cases, and theories derived by induction from previous particular cases – that a solution can be reached which is in harmony with the whole international legal order.

For these reasons, while Professor d'Amato's study and reformulation of the theory of international customary law is of undoubted value in focussing attention on the need for any theory on the subject to be based, in the last resort, on what States actually do, and on what impact customary rules have *on them*, we do not propose to adopt the suggested reformulation of the theory for the purposes of our consideration of the relationship of customary law to codification and to codified law.]

The mention above of what may be called the "single-element" theory of the formation of custom, namely the theory that general and consistent practice is sufficient to create legally binding custom without proof of any particular psychological attitude, suggests a further approach to the question. The principal objection to the "single-element" theory, as already mentioned, is that it affords no means of distinguishing between usages which give rise to legally binding custom, and usages which remain in the sphere of mere courtesy or convenience; but to make it possible to make this distinction it is not necessary to assert the existence (or non-existence) of a belief by the States concerned that they are following existing law. Would it not be an answer to Kelsen's objection to the traditional theory, and at the same time nearer to the likely truth of the way in which customs do in fact develop, to say that the requirement of *opinio juris* is equivalent merely to the need for the practice in question to have been accompanied by

24. A.J.P. Tammes, The Inter-action of the Sources of International Law, *X Nederlands Tijdschrift* (1963), p. 225, at p. 234.

either a sense of conforming with the law, or the view that the practice was potentially law, as suited to the needs of the international community, and not a mere matter of convenience or courtesy? The psychological element would thus also include the view that if the practice in question was not required by the law, it was in the process of becoming so.[25]

The influence of Verdross[26] and of Charles de Visscher[27] will be observed at this point: but the view here advanced does not entirely correspond either to the former's theory of the *opinio juris* as the consciousness of helping a principle of law which has not yet become positive law to assert itself, or to the latter's view that the process is one of recognition by States that the rule in question corresponds to an implementation of the underlying basic principles of their society.[28] This essentially naturalistic approach has been criticised[29] in that it implies the progressive discovery by States of the *pre-existing* rules which correspond to their social needs, which is undeniably a rather artificial view of the process involved, particularly when the field of activity to be governed by the emerging rule is one which is entirely new, such as the exploration of space.

Without necessarily wishing to exclude the natural-law approach – since it is difficult to contend that the rules in fact chosen by States to meet the needs of their conflicting interests will not be, or correspond closely to, the rules which theoretically could have been laid down from the beginning by an omniscient legislator – we may perhaps lay greater stress on the subjective nature of the process, implied by the word *opinio*. What in fact is here suggested is that what counts is the view held by a State of its

25. Cf. Dissenting Opinion of Judge Lachs, *Continental Shelf* cases, *I.C.J. Reports 1969*, p. 218, at pp. 230-231: "[Other States] may also have been convinced that the instrument . . . was intended to become and would in due course become general law (the teleological element is of no small importance in the formation of law)".

26. The view that States act consciously "eine ausserrechtliche Norm anzuwenden oder eine solche zu pozitivieren, die für den zwischenstaatlichen Verkehr notwendig ist": *Völkerrecht*, p. 138; [cf. also Verdross, Das Völkerrechtliche Gewohnheitsrecht. *Japanese Annual of International Law*, 1963.]

27. See 6 *Recueil des Cours*, 1925-I, p. 325, at pp. 349-353.

28. ". . . une règle issue de la pratique internationale devient coutumière, devient règle de droit, lorsque la généralité des Etats la considère comme la sanction nécessaire des règles normatives ou primaires qui sont à la base de leurs relations mutuelles." De Visscher, *op. cit.*, 6 Recueil des Cours, at p. 353.

29. Notably by Kunz in 47 *A.J.I.L.* (1953), p. 662 at p. 667.

own conduct in relation to the law, not the absolute social desirability of their conduct. If a State considers – rightly or wrongly – either that an existing rule of law requires it to act in a certain way, or that a particular course of action is of such a kind that its recognition as in accordance with law, *de lege ferenda*, would be socially desirable, then this is sufficient (if the view is or becomes general) to distinguish the emerging legal rule from the usage, or potential usage, of courtesy or convenience.[30]

It may be asked whether, on the theory here discussed, the practice of States accompanied only by the view that the practice in question should be or become – *de lege ferenda* – a rule of general international law is sufficient of itself to generate a rule of customary law, or whether it merely suffices to start the process of adoption of the practice by the law, and must be followed by at least some practice accompanied by the view that the rule exists, – *de lege lata* – for the practice to become part of the general law. Such an interpretation would make it possible to take early practice into account in assessing the generality and the consistency of usage, while still requiring some degree of *opinio juris* in the traditional sense in addition. Something of the sort has undoubtedly been the practice of international tribunals faced with problems of the existence or non-existence of rules of customary law.

It will however be observed that such an interpretation fails to escape the logical dilemma to which attention has been drawn by Kelsen. Only if the view that the custom *should* be law has the effect of making it law (provided it is coupled with sufficiently general usage), can subsequent practice be coupled with the correct view that the custom *is* law.

In effect, this view involves the reversal, chronologically speaking, of the expression *opinio juris sive necessitatis*, and entails considering that the States which initiate the practice which is to grow into a rule of customary international law act under the influence of an *opinio necessitatis* – but an opinion that the practice in question is necessary *as law*, not merely as a matter of convenience –, and that as a result of such practice a legal rule

30. Cf. the discussion by the I.C.J. of the way in which the "equidistance rule" became incorporated into the 1958 Geneva Convention on the Continental Shelf, and the Court's conclusion that it was not a potential rule of customary law: *I.C.J. Reports 1969*, p. 3, at pp. 37-41.

comes into being, so that States subsequently acting in accordance with it can be said to be acting in accordance with *opinio juris* in the strictest sense. The *opinio necessitatis* in the early stages is sufficient to create a rule of law, but its continued existence is dependent on subsequent practice accompanied by *opinio juris*, failing which the new-born rule will prove a sickly infant, and fail to survive for long. It is suggested that whatever the theoretical merits of this construction,[31] it does reflect reality in that there must be some qualitative difference between the psychological accompaniment of the first examples of a given practice and that of subsequent repeated instances.[32]

One clarification should perhaps be added at this stage. It is not suggested that any mere general co-incidence of views among States, that a given practice should be a matter of international law, is enough, unless the practice is in fact followed sufficiently consistently by a sufficient number of States. In other words the interpretation of the *opinio juris* discussed above is not intended to do away with the additional requirement of practice or usage, the material element in the formation of customary law. Any attempt to base its authority solely on the consent of States, without requiring that such consent be incarnated in the form of actual practice runs into the difficulty that if consent is sufficient, consent is required as a basis for customary law; therefore there is no justification for holding that customary law is binding on new States.[33] Furthermore, States express their consent to be bound by a rule, e.g. by ratifying a treaty, or in appropriate circumstances by other means, such as a unilateral declaration,[34] only through certain State organs or officials authorized to bind the state; and therefore it would not be legitimate to regard other acts

31. ["Legal theories are the creation of the human mind. The jurist who proposes a new theory wants us to believe that the facts . . . correspond to his abstractions. Unfortunately this is not always the case . . ." (Schmitthof in 129 *Recueil des Cours*, 1970-I, p. 115)].

32. [To recognise this need not entail going so far as to divide States into two classes, those who *make* the new law, and those who merely *comply* with it and to deny the need for *opinio juris sive necessitatis* so far as the second class is concerned (cf. Mokre, *Theorie des Gewohnheitsrechts,* 1932, at pp. 191-192, quoted by Zemanek in *Festschrift Verdross*, p. 590.]

33. This is the difficulty of the theory advanced by Strupp of the *pactum tacitum*: see 47 *Recueil des Cours* 1934-I, p. 263.

34. Cf the "Ihlen Declaration" in the *Eastern Greenland* case: *P.C.I.J. Series A/B No. 53.*

of or on behalf of States as elements of practice required by traditional law for the creation of a customary rule. Thus the argument in favour of "instant custom"[35] renders unworkable the normal process by which the existence of a customary rule is deduced and pieced together from widely varying types of acts which can be classified as the practice of States.[36]

This point is important because it is not always easy to distinguish, in a discussion *in abstracto*, between the statement that such and such a rule is law and such and such a rule should be law, as the records of the International Law Commission make abundantly clear. When considering State practice from the standpoint of customary law as obligation, emphasised by Mr. MacGibbon, and in particular the obligation of acquiescence or non-objection by States affected by the conduct of the State which asserts a claim based on customary law, the fact that the practice is "against interest" gives it more weight than the mere acceptance of a theoretical rule in the course of discussion by State representatives at a conference, and considerably more weight than the assertion of such a rule. The importance of this will emerge from our discussion of the concept of "international legislation" as an expression of customary law.

This brings us to the question of the nature of the other element required for the creation of international custom, the material element variously described by the International Court as "la pratique internationale constante", "consistent international practice", "la tradition constante", "unvarying tradition", "usage constant", "constant and uniform practice", etc.[37]

The very real distinction which must be emphasised in this connection is that between the practice of States, which constitutes the material element of custom, and evidence of the practice of States which is not itself practice. The distinction is no less vital for being not infrequently extremely difficult to make with regard to a given set of facts advanced in support of a claim as to the existence of a rule of international customary law.

35. Dr. Bin Cheng's expression: see below, p. 72.

36. See Barberis, L'élément matériel de la coutume internationale d'après la Cour de La Haye (1922-1966), XIV *Nederlands Tijdschrift* (1967) 367.

37. See Barberis, L'élément matériel de la coutume internationale d'après la Cour de La Haye, XIV *Nederlands Tijdschrift* (1967) p. 367, at p. 380, and the references there given.

The substance of the practice required is that States have done, or abstained from doing, certain things in the international field: e.g., that they have exercised diplomatic protection in certain circumstances, or recognised the rights of other States to do so; that they have refrained from bringing or permitting legal proceedings against visiting diplomats;[38] that they have claimed certain rights over certain areas of submarine territory, or recognised such rights claimed by other States. State practice as the material element in the formation of custom is, it is worth emphasising, *material*: it is composed of acts by States with regard to a particular person, ship, defined area of territory, each of which amounts to the assertion or repudiation of a claim relating to a particular apple of discord. Claims may be made in the widest of general terms; but the occasion of an act of State practice contributing to the formation of custom must always be some specific dispute or potential dispute.

The mere assertion *in abstracto* of the existence of a legal right or legal rule is not an act of State practice; but it may be adduced as evidence of the acceptance by the State against which it is sought to set up a claim, of the customary rule which is alleged to exist, assuming that that State asserts that it is not bound by the alleged rule.[39] More important, such assertions can be relied on as *supplementary* evidence both of State practice and of the existence of the *opinio juris*; but only as supplementary evidence, and not as one element to be included in the summing up of State practice for the purpose of assessing its generality.

Practice or usage consists of an accumulation of acts which are material or concrete in the sense that they are intended to have an immediate effect on the legal relationships of the State concerned; and acts which are relevant only as assertions in the abstract, such as the recognition by a representative of a State at a diplomatic conference that an alleged rule exists are not constitutive of practice and thus of custom, but only confirmatory of it. The only apparent exception to this principle – which is not really an exception – is the act of a State in ratifying or acceding to a

38. Sørensen points out that this is an example of abstention resulting from a positive decision, capable of contributing to the growth of customary law: *Les sources du droit international*, pp. 98-99.

39. E.g., by virtue of historic title or consistent protest: cf. the contentions of Norway in the *Fisheries* case, *I.C.J. Reports 1951*, p. 116 (and see below, p. 112).

multilateral treaty which directly or indirectly asserts the existence, at least for the future and for the States parties to the treaty, of a rule of law. Just as a series of bilateral treaties concluded over a period of time by various States, all consistently adopting the same solution to the same problem of the relationships between them, may give rise to a new rule of customary international law, so the general ratification of a treaty laying down general rules to govern the future relationships of States in a given field has a similar effect. The practice here is concrete in the sense that each State does not merely assert the desirability, or even the existence, of the rule of law in question, but by a definite and formal decision accepts the rule for the regulation of its own interests in future differences in the field covered by the treaty. For this reason, it is possible, as the International Court of Justice stated in the *North Sea Continental Shelf* cases,[40] for a custom to arise simply from the general (but not universal) ratification of a codifying treaty.

It will be noted that this view of the formation of custom, whereby universal or general acceptance of a treaty may form a custom but universal or general declaration *in abstracto* of the existence of a rule will not, cannot be reconciled with the theory of Strupp and others,[41] which regards the formation of custom as purely the operation of the consent of States (*pactum tacitum*). If the essential element in the formation of international customary law were that of the consent of States, there would be no reason why such consent could not be given to a new rule of law in the abstract; provided of course such consent were expressed by the competent representatives or organs of each State concerned. Law so created would however hardly deserve the appellation of "customary law"; for reasons already touched on,[42] the *pactum tacitum* theory, which under-rates the importance of the immediate and concrete aspect of State practice, does not appear to us to be appropriate to the facts of the creation of law by international intercourse.

A further problem, general in its scope, concerning the nature and formation of customary international law which will prove to be relevant to our study, is that of the nature of local, regional, or

40. *I.C.J. Reports 1969*, p. 3, at p. 42, para. 73.
41. See Règles générales de la paix, 47 *Recueil des Cours*, 1934-I, p. 263ff.
42. Above, pp. 4-5, 56.

special customary law. For reasons of practical convenience, however, we propose to reserve the examination of this problem until it arises in connection with our examination of the development of law after the conclusion of a general codifying treaty.[43]

43. See below, p. 135.

Chapter Five

INTERNATIONAL LEGISLATION THROUGH THE UNITED NATIONS

We have already discussed the use of the term "international legislation" by Manley Hudson and others[1] to refer to the development of law by means of the multilateral codifying treaty, and have remarked on the impossibility of the creation *ex nihilo* of a new source of law more closely related to the concept of a legislator on the municipal level,[2] that is to say the impossibility of legislation acquiring the rank of a source of law other than through the operation of one or more of the existing sources. We must now turn to the claims made for the resolutions and declarations of the General Assembly of the United Nations as a "legislative" activity as effective as multilateral treaties for the creation of generally binding rules of law, and in its nature better entitled to the name of legislation.

The legal significance of such resolutions or declarations is however here examined solely from the point of view of their claim to embody or enact general international law. We are therefore not concerned with the legal effect of what we may call particular resolutions, that is to say resolutions having a specific addressee, named or implied, and deciding, recommending or requiring something specific. There are good reasons for attributing to such acts, even when expressed in the form of a recommendation, a considerable degree of legal effectiveness[3] ; but such reasons do not apply in any way when the acts of the Assembly under study are, or purport to be, legislative on a universal scale.

It must be conceded at the outset that many authors who in

1. See the quotation from Hudson's book of that title, above, p. 25, note 34.
2. See above, p. 39.
3. See in particular the argument of Judge Lauterpacht, *South West Africa (Voting Procedure), I.C.J. Reports 1955*, p. 90, at p. 118-9.

fact consider the law-making activities of the General Assembly of the United Nations to be more effective than the present writer is inclined, for reasons to be given in this Chapter, to accept, do not use the term "international legislation" to refer to such activities. Thus for example, Dr. Rosalyn Higgins states clearly in the introduction to her exhaustive study of the subject that

> "... the Assembly certainly has no right to legislate in the commonly understood sense of the term. Resolutions of the Assembly are not *per se* binding: though those rules of general international law which they may embody are binding on member States, with or without the help of the resolution".[4]

Thus it must be emphasised that it is we who have chosen the term to refer to this particular method of law-creation, simply as a convenient means of reference, and without in any way implying that those who regard the effects of General Assembly resolutions as lawmaking are being misled by a transposition of the municipal term "legislation" to the international plane.

[A "quasi-legislative effect" has also been claimed for the resolutions of the General Assembly, in particular by Professor Richard Falk;[5] this contention is not here examined, because despite the use of the term "quasi-legislative",[6] the effect to which Professor Falk has rightly drawn attention is rather one of persuasiveness than one which can be attributed to a law-making activity as such, and as the term is used in the present study. Professor Falk's approach has in fact much in common with that of Professor d'Amato, discussed earlier;[7] and all that need be said here is that it is important not to let the term "quasi-legislative", which for Professor Falk has a clear but very limited content, and is consistently applied by him, be used to cover confused thinking about the effects of such resolutions upon and according to customary law.]

The question of the general legal effect of declarations – in which term is included all formal statements of a legal nature and purporting to express legal rules binding on States, whether entitled resolutions, declarations or whatever, which are not em-

4. *The Development of International Law through the Political Organs of the United Nations* (1963), p. 5.

5. [On the Quasi-legislative Competence of the General Assembly, 60 A.J.I.L. (1966), p. 782.]

6. [On the dangers of the "question-begging term 'quasi' "which is "*ex hypothesi* an evasion", see C.K. Allen, *Law and Orders*, p. 390.]

7. [supra, pp. 49ff.]

bodied in a treaty-document to which States are invited to express their specific assent in the normal way – has really only arisen since the creation of the United Nations Organization. The Council and the Assembly of the League of Nations did not themselves attempt to declare, create, or codify law, and the reports of the Commissions of Jurists set up from time to time by the League from time to time on particular problems,[8] although of a persuasive authority to some extent comparable with the advisory opinions of the Permanent Court of International Justice, were not intended as general statements of law for future guidance.

We are not here concerned with the resolutions and declarations of such bodies as the Institut de droit international, which, however authoritative in themselves, are not international organisations of States. A resolutions of the Institut is of great persuasive authority and evidential value as to the state of international law on the point in question, provided that it is clear that it is expressed *de lege lata*; and a resolution which is clearly intended to express the views of those adopting it *de lege ferenda* may well contribute to the development of customary law, and as such subsequently be relied on to show the course upon which such development was directed. However, such resolutions cannot constitute the practice of States, nor, beyond a certain point, confirm the existence of the *opinio juris* with regard to an existing practice of which there is evidence available from other sources.

An author who is strongly in favour of attributing to Declarations of the United Nations General Assembly the force of binding international law, for a number of (not entirely consistent) reasons is Mr. O.Y. Asamoah; and it will be convenient to take as a starting point his discussion of the relationship of General Assembly Declarations with customary law.[9]

It is contended first that resolutions of the General Assembly may constitute the practice of States; secondly that they may originate practice; thirdly that they may corroborate customary

8. E.g. the Commisstion set up – before the establishment of the Permanent Court of International Justice – to advise on the Åaland Islands question (L. of N. Off. J., 1920, Special Supplement, p. 3), and the Commission which advised on the Monod case (L. of N. Off. J., 1925, p. 144), and which may be said to have been the forerunner of the Administrative Tribunals of the League and of the United Nations.

9. O.Y. Asamoah, *The Legal Significance of the Declarations of the General Assembly of the United Nations,* pp. 46ff.

rules of international law; and fourthly that, in appropriate cases, they may supply the *opinio juris sive necessitatis.*[10]

The second of these possibilities need not detain us at this point; it is certainly the case that a statement by the Assembly of principles or rules suitable for application to a given field may well give rise to a practice which may grow, possibly in quite a short time, into a rule or set of rules of customary law. This however has nothing to do with the lawmaking qualities of the resolution as such: the same result might equally follow, as just noted, from a statement of rules *de lege ferenda* by a wholly unofficial body such as the Institut de droit international. The principles or rules which eventually emerge as part of customary law will owe their force as law entirely to the two basic elements of customary law – usage and *opinio juris* – and only their formulation to the Assembly resolution. Thus, assuming that the final rules tally in all respects with the rules expressed in the resolution, what will have happened will be a reversal of a codifying operation: instead of the resolution having formulated in orderly and written form the rules which have developed by practice, practice will have adopted the rules put forward, and will in all probability have done so partly because in addition to suiting the subject matter, they present the advantage of order and ease of reference.

The possibility that resolutions of the General Assembly may corroborate other evidence tending to show the existence of a rule of customary international law also does not go to the nature of the resolution itself as an element of international law.[11] It is certain that an international tribunal called upon to determine the existence of a customary rule would take account of any relevant

10. There are at least two other possible bases on which it might be claimed that United Nations resolutions are "lawmaking", namely as authoritative interpretation of the Charter (Asamoah, *op. cit.*, p. 42ff.) and as statements of "general principles of law" (Article 38 (i) (c) of the I.C.J. Statute) (*ibid.* p. 61ff.). On this last point, Verdross, Kann die Generalversammlung der Vereinten Nationen das Völkerrecht weiterbilden?, 26 *Zeitschrift* (1966) p. 690 at p. 695, who argues that a two-thirds majority (including the permanent members of the Security Council) must recognise the principle "durch ihre Praxis oder ausdrücklich". (Contra, R. Higgins, *The Development of International Law through the Political Organs of the United Nations,* p. 6.). These arguments are, however, not material to our discussion here.

11. As Verdross observes, a resolution operating in this way, or originating State practice (see previous paragraph) is only a material source of law and not a formal source. Verdross, Kann die Generalversammlung der Vereinten Nationen das Völkerrecht weiterbilden?,, 26 *Zeitschrift* (1966), p. 690 at p. 693.

resolution of the Assembly and of the discussions leading up to it.[12] It is suggested, however, that in fact the discussions, and the statements made on behalf of member States made in the discussions, will almost always be of greater relevance than the final resolution.[13] This is a distinction which is of some importance in connection with the other aspects of Mr. Asamoah's thesis, and it should perhaps therefore be emphasized.

It cannot be denied that when a resolution is formally adopted in so universal an organisation as the United Nations, the resolution is something more than the consistent statements or wishes of the member States; that, in a sense, the whole is more than the sum of its parts. However it is easy to attach too much importance to the resolution, and too little to the positions taken up by States which have contributed to its adoption, apart from the States which have opposed it but, being in a minority, have not affected its creation. It is essential to consider each possible type of resolution, if not each resolution on its merits, since the relative weight of the resolution itself and of the positions of Member States will vary according to the form and subject matter of the resolution in question.

It is obvious that purely procedural decisions in the form of resolutions, and decisions affecting the working of the United Nations as an organisation, such as the adoption of the budget or the election of the Secretary-General, are in a different class from the sort of resolution we are dealing with.[14] When decisions of the kind just mentioned are taken, the resolution is all, and the role of States is irrelevant; the Secretary-General is elected, or the budget is adopted, by an act of the Organisation, and the reasons why certain States voted against, and the fact that they did so, are of no importance. The resolution expresses the will of the organisa-

12. Cf. *International Status of South West Africa, I.C.J. Reports 1950,* pp. 134-135, with regard to a League of Nations resolution and the statements of South Africa; this is, however, a question involving a League institution (the Mandate) and not questions of general international law.

13. As Sørensen says, "il s'agit d'actes imputables aux Etats agissant par l'intermédiaire de leurs representants, plutôt que d'actes imputables à l'organe international en tant que tel". 101 *Recueil des Cours,* 1960-III, p. 38.

14. See Basak, *Decisions of the United Nations Organs in the Judgments and Opinions of the International Court of Justice,* (Wroclaw, 1969), particularly pp. 39ff; [Bleicher, The Legal Significance of Re-citation of General Assembly Resolutions, 63 A.J.I.L. (1969), at p. 445.]

tion in a field where the wills of the individual States can have no effect by themselves.

On the other hand, where what is in question is a matter of existing, or nascent, or potential customary law, the wills of the individual States are highly relevant, and can themselves contribute to the creation or development of law. The will, and for that matter, the practice, of the Organisation, on the other hand is not relevant, unless the field is one in which the organisation as a subject of international law is directly interested as an organisation, e.g. in the field of compensation for injury to agents of the organisation.[15] In other fields, with regard to, let us say, the law of the sea, the will of the organisation is only of interest if it can be regarded as the jointly expressed will of the member States, or of a majority of them; and in such a case, what is really of interest is the size and composition of the majority (e.g. in a matter affecting the high seas, were the principal maritime States in favour?) and the proportionate size of the minority.

This observation is true where the question is one of the evidential value of a resolution in support of an alleged rule of customary law based principally on practice of States outside the meeting-hall of the Assembly, but, as we shall see, it is also of importance in connection with the suggestion that Assembly resolutions can themselves constitute practice of States, or express the *opinio juris*, so as to be creative of customary law.

There would appear to be no objection of theory to the assertion that a General Assembly resolution may be evidence of the *opinio juris* with regard to a practice of which there is, apart from the resolution itself, adequate evidence of usage. It is in this way, and probably only in this way, that weight can be attached to the resolution itself, rather than to the multiple consents involved in its adoption by States; if a resolution stating or declaring the state of the law on a given subject is adopted by a sufficient majority to be regarded as generally representative, and provided the majority does not exclude the States most directly concerned, then it will probably be impossible to challenge the authority of the rules so stated on the ground that the *opinio juris* is lacking or unproved.

15. Compare the position of the International Court of Justice in the *Reparation for Injuries* case (*I.C.J. Reports 1949,* p. 174) with its refusal to attach legal significance to UN administrative practice in the *Reservations to the Genocide Convention* case (*I.C.J. Reports 1951,* p. 15 at pp. 25-26).

This however presupposes a sufficient body of State practice for the usage element of the alleged custom to be established without reference to the resolution; and if there is such practice, it will be comparatively rare for it to be necessary to have resort to a resolution or declaration to show the existence of the psychological element, since this also will probably emerge from the evidence otherwise available.

Of far greater practical importance, therefore, if proved, is the contention that the adoption of a resolution declaring or stating the law can itself constitute the necessary practice. If this argument is accepted, the question of resolutions as evidence of *opinio juris* becomes practically academic, since States which solemnly declare certain rules to be law, in the knowledge that by doing so they make them law so far as the requirement of practice is concerned, must be taken to know and intend those rules to be binding. This of course involves a wide interpretation of the psychological element of custom: according to the traditional interpretation, the *opinio juris,* in relation to a given practice, means the consciousness, while acting or refraining from acting, so as to follow the practice, that to act or to refrain from acting, as the case may be, is required by customary law.[16] If however we accept for the sake of argument that to vote for a resolution declaring the law on, let us say, diplomatic immunities, is an act of State practice contributing to the affirmation of the law of diplomatic immunities, we must apparently say that customary law on diplomatic immunities requires States to vote in favour of any resolution of an international organ which declares the law on the subject.[17] On any traditional interpretation, the only rule which could be created by the combination of *opinio juris* and voting in the General Assembly, the act of voting constituting practice, would be a rule imposing, in certain circumstances, a duty to cast an affirmative vote in the General Assembly, which would be a rule without much practical content.

16. See above, p. 47.

17. This rather curious conclusion does, it is true, seem to follow *a contrario* from the assertion that a limited number of votes for a codifying resolution, or a limited number of ratifications of a codifying treaty, can be treated as evidence that the resolution or treaty did not declare existing international law. Cf., for example, in the *Asylum* case: "It is contended that this Convention has merely codified principles which were already recognized by Latin-American custom . . . The limited number of States which have ratified this Convention reveals the weakness of this argument . . ." *I.C.J. Reports 1950*, p. 277. On "negative *opinio juris*", see below p. 116.

We thus touch on the basic difficulty to which the contention that resolutions may constitute State practice gives rise. In analysing a set of facts put forward in support of an alleged rule of customary law, it is easy to blur the distinction between the practical element and evidence of the psychological element in custom: in many cases, the two are not distinguishable. A State which asserts the existence of a right to which it claims to be entitled is simultaneously contributing a formal act to the corpus of practice on the subject, and asserting its view that the matter is one of law, not of convenience, courtesy or unsettled practice, and that its claim is co-terminous with its right[18] and thus providing evidence of the *opinio juris.* Nevertheless, it is suggested that it is essential to make the distinction, and to decline to admit into the body of the law, not only alleged rules which rest only on practice with no evidence of the belief of States in their obligatory nature, but also rules which, although widely regarded as binding in law, have never in fact been applied in practice. This is not to say that such rules cannot exist, that all rules of law must have their roots in the soil of actual usage, but only that it is of the essence of a *customary* rules to be firmly earthbound, built upon a foundation of actual experience in the relations of States. The "general principles of law" referred to in Article 38 (1) (c) of the Statute of the International Court of Justice exist in a more rarefied air; and it is always possible for new rules, never applied, and possibly never capable of application, to be created by international agreement, and possibly even by universally subscribed declaration: but such rules are not, and cannot be, regarded as customary law, without depriving the title of all significance.

This last difficulty is the principal objection to a more moderate position than Mr. Asamoah's, namely that of Professor Sørensen; the latter raises directly the question whether a resolution of the General Assembly is anything more than evidence of the existence of the *opinio juris,* and continues

> "En d'autres termes, faut-il prouver en outre que la norme formulée par la résolution correspond à une pratique générale des Etats? Le caractère formel et institutionalisé de l'expression juridique nous dispense, à mon avis, de cette preuve".[19]

Thus Professor Sørensen makes the distinction, which it is sug-

18. See above, p. 49.
19. Principes de droit international public, 101 *Recueil des Cours,* 1960-III, at p. 99.

gested is vital, between acts actually constituting State practice and those which are only relevant as evidence of the belief that a rule of law is involved, and recognises that a resolution cannot of itself constitute practice; his argument is apparently either to the effect that practice is wholly unnecessary, which leads ineluctably to the conclusion that an Assembly resolution is a source of law *sui generis*, and not a particular aspect or expression of customary law; or to the effect that the resolution creates a presumption – that it renders proof of practice unnecessary – in effect a presumption that the rule embodied in the resolution has passed into general law as supported by State practice.

If the latter is the correct understanding of the argument, one may enquire whether the presumption in question is an absolute one, or whether it may be overthrown by the production of evidence either of lack of practice, or of practice conflicting with the terms of the resolution. If the first interpretation – that the presumption is absolute – is to be preferred, then the problem is, as already mentioned, how this new source of law came to be part of positive law: for a rule that a resolution of the General Assembly may create an absolute presumption in favour of what it lays down as the law is hardly distinguishable from a rule that a resolution of the General Assembly creates law, *tout court*. It would seem that Professor Sørensen does not intend to go as far as this, namely to claim for General Assembly resolutions the status of a source of law *sui generis*, for a little further on in his Hague lectures he seems to withdraw somewhat from his original position, by summing up the question in these terms:

> "Par conséquent, il faut se mettre en garde contre toute tendance à attribuer à l'Assemblée générale un pouvoir législatif dans les matières qui ne relèvent pas du droit interne de l'organisation.[20] Par ses résolutions elle peut affirmer le droit existant et lui donner une expression qui fait autorité. Elle peut également contribuer à la cristallisation d'une norme coutumière qui se dessine déjà vaguement dans la pratique, mais elle ne peut pas modifier le droit existant ou créer de nouvelles règles".[21]

The expression "crystallisation" of a customary rule is one which was much used in the Continental Shelf cases before the Interna-

20. Cf. R. Higgins, *The Development of International Law though the Political Organs of the United Nations*, p. 5: ". . . the Assembly certainly has no right to legislate in the commonly understood sense of the term".

21. 101 *Recueil des Cours*, 1960-III, p. 100.

tional Court of Justice[22] in 1968-69, and is a useful, and apparently fairly recent, addition to the terminology of the subject.

It can certainly be accepted that a General Assembly resolution may contribute to the crystallisation process, and that the existence of such a resolution declaring, or purporting to declare, the law will require only comparatively slight evidence of actual practice to support the conclusion that the rule in question has passed into general customary law. Nevertheless it must be emphasized that the Assembly cannot change the law or create new law; and as Professor Sørensen concludes:

> "... l'effet d'une résolution dans ce domaine est plutôt déclaratoire que constitutif".[23]

A convenient recent example of a resolution of the General Assembly which is clearly designed to be "codifying" *lato sensu* is the 1963 Declaration of Legal Principles Governing the activities of States in the Exploration and Use of Outer Space.[24] The resolution embodying the Declaration was adopted unanimously,[25] and it is as solemn an enunciation of the legal principles in a given field as the General Assembly has ever given, so that from these two points of view its claim to rank as a legislative act is a strong one.

Yet there are two good reasons why it is difficult to regard the Declaration, as does for example, Dr. Jenks,[26] as an expression or codification of customary law with regard to the exploration and use of outer space. In the first place, the opening words of the operative part of the resolution are "Solemnly declares that in the exploration and use of outer space States *should* be guided by the following principles".[27] Of this, Mr. H.G. Darwin observes, rather mysteriously, that the wording "falls short of purporting to create existing law".[28] The idea of law being *created* by a General Assembly resolution is, as we have seen, inappropriate except in certain limited fields linked with the Charter; but is the wording

22. In which Professor Sørensen sat as judge *ad hoc*, and contributed a stimulating Dissenting Opinion.
23. 101 *Recueil des Cours,* 1960-III, p. 100.
24. Resolution 1962 (XVIII) of 13 December 1963.
25. See U.N. Doc. A/PV.1280.
26. *A New World of Law*? , p. 146; see also the same author's *Space Law,* p. 185.
27. Italics added: cf. French text: "... les Etats *devraient* être guidés ..."
28. H.G. Darwin, The Outer Space Treaty, 42 *B.Y.I.L.* (1967) p. 278 at p. 280.

appropriate to *declare* what is claimed to be existing law? In the light of the observations of the representatives of various member States, quoted by Mr. Darwin, it does not appear that such an interpretation is possible.[29]

But the second and more important reason why it is doubtful whether the 1963 Declaration can be regarded as an expression of existing customary law is because custom, as we have endeavoured to show, requires a certain amount of actual State practice to give it life and substance: and opportunities for practice in outer space prior to 1963 – and even since that date – have been sparse indeed. The vital paragraph 3 of the Declaration, providing that

> "Outer space and celestial bodies are not subject to national appropriation by claim of sovereignty, by means of use and occupation, or by any other means"

could be regarded as based on the practice of two States only, which had, at the time of the 1963 Declaration, made no more progress towards "use and occupation" of any celestial body than the projection of unmanned vehicles to the moon. While it is true that in regard to a branch of law of this kind, very little practice might be regarded as sufficient, and that the fact of only two States being at present in a position to contribute to the practice implies that the practice of those two states would, if it were consistent enough, be sufficient, it is suggested that at the date of the 1963 Declaration it was quite impossible to speak of usages which had crystallised into rules of customary international law. Writing in 1967, Mr. Darwin was unconvinced that even the practice of the additional four years which had then elapsed, after the stimulus of the Declaration itself, could be sufficient to ground a rule of law.[30]

The Outer Space Treaty of 1965, on the other hand, could more easily pass into general law; as the International Court observed with regard to the 1958 Geneva Convention on the Continental Shelf,

29. In this sense, see [Suzanne Bastid, Observations sur une "étape" dans le développement progressif de la codification des principes du droit internation, *En hommage à Paul Guggenheim,* p. 132 at pp. 138-9;] D. Goedhuis, Reflections on the Evolution of Space Law, *XIII Nederlands Tijdschrift* (1966), p. 109 at p. 111. Professor Goedhuis is however opposed to the general views advanced in the present study as to the need for practice as well as *opinio juris* for the establishment of a customary law rule, even one embodied in a resolution: *ibid.,* p. 113.

30. 42 *B.Y.I.L.* (1967), at p. 281.

"... a very widespread and representative participation in the convention might suffice of itself, provided it included that of States whose interests were specially affected".[31]

In this context, the States whose interests are specially affected would presumably be those which are actually or potentially in control of the economic and scientific assets necessary for the exploration of space. In this particular field, indeed, it might be unnecessary to look much beyond such States; the difficult problem, to which M. Jack Lang has drawn attention,[32] of deciding just what is "widespread" and "representative" participation in a given convention, may in this particular case be unusually simple to resolve, since many of the provisions of the treaty cannot be regarded as affecting the interests of the smaller and economically less well-developed States to more than an infinitesimal extent.[33]

It is in connection with the law of outer space that Dr. Bin Cheng has adopted a more radical approach even than that of Mr. Asamoah to the question of law-making effect of General Assembly resolutions; Dr. Cheng's appraoch might be regarded as the complete reversal, or the mirror-image, of the "single element" theory of the creation of custom[34] advanced by Kelsen and Guggenheim. Where the latter writers have contended that State practice is sufficient to produce a rule of customary law, and the psychological element does not also have to be proved to exist (*corpus* without *animus*), Dr. Cheng has argued that the *opinio juris*, if sufficiently generally held, is sufficient without any need for practice in support (*animus* without *corpus*), or more precisely that the *corpus* of State practice is only required to prove the existence of the *animus,* and is therefore unnecessary if the latter can be proved by other means.[35]

"Indeed, it may be permissible to ... say that the role of usage in the establishment of rules of international customary law is purely evidentiary: it provides evidence on the one hand of the contents of the rule in question and on the other hand of the *opinio juris* of the States concerned. Not only is it unnecessary that the usage should be prolonged, but there need also be no usage at all in the sense

31. *I.C.J. Reports 1969*, p. 42, para. 73. See p. 85 below.

32. *Le Plateau continental de la Mer du Nord,* pp. 105-110.

33. [Except as regards the implications of such involuntary participation in space exploration as the reception of a fallen satellite on their territory: cf. the obligation to return such strays laid down in article 7 of the Declaration.]

34. See above, pp. 47-48.

35. [According to Quadri in 113 *Recueil des Cours* 1964-III, p. 326, this view is one which has been held by certain recent Italian authors also.]

of repeated practice, provided that the *opinio juris* of the States concerned can be clearly established. Consequently, international customary law has in reality only one constitutive element, the *opinio juris*. Where there is *opinio juris*, there is a rule of international customary law".[36]

The position of the present writer on the question of the formative elements of international custom has already been made clear: as Dr. Cheng himself concedes,

"... in the case of a rule without usage, objection might be taken to the use of the term custom or customary".

Some degree of actual usage in the sense of application of the alleged rule to concrete situations of fact would, in our view, be necessary for an abstract rule of law, stated *de lege ferenda*, to become binding international law, *lex lata*; or, at the very least, a clear intention on the part of the generality of States to make the rule law by ratifying a treaty containing it. Even this last process, which has the blessing of the International Court, comes near to contradicting the significance of the expression "customary law"; and it does not seem sufficient to dismiss the objection airily as Dr. Cheng does by saying that

"whether in such a case one speaks of international customary law or an unwritten rule of international law becomes purely a matter of terminology".[37]

This only prompts the question, what are these unwritten rules of international law, and whence do they come? If they are not in fact rules of customary law – which on the traditional interpretation of the process of formation of such rules, they cannot be, – nor the effective application of the "general principles of law" (which in any case it is arguable are only a source of law for tribunals which would otherwise be forced to declare a *non liquet*),[38] they must be a new sort of international law, derived

36. B. Cheng, United Nations Resolutions on Outer Space: "Instant" International Customary Law? , *V Indian Journal of International Law,* January 1965, p. 23; quotations from p. 36. The same approach is adopted by Prof. Goedhuis, Reflections on the Evolution of Space Law, *XIII Nederlands Tijdschrift* (1966), p. 109 at p. 113, [and The International Law Association and the Development of a Legal Regime of Outer Space, in *New Frontiers in Space Law,* (Sijthoff/Oceana, 1969), at pp. 33-34.]

37. *Op. cit.,* p. 36.

38. See [the discussions of the Advisory Committee of Jurists on the P.C.I.J. Statute, e.g., at pp. 296,] Siorat, *Le problème des lacunes en droit international*; Lauterpacht, Some Observations on the Problem of *Non Liquet* and the Completeness of the Legal Order, in *Symbolae Verzijl,* p. 196; Stone, *Non Liquet* and the Function of Law in the International Community, 35 *B.Y.I.L.* (1959) p. 124.

from a new source, presumably some kind of international legislation.

The basis and justification for such a legislative power in resolutions such as the 1963 Declaration on Outer Space is, in Dr. Cheng's argument, essentially a voluntarist approach:

> "... the possibility of international customary law without usage becomes obvious if it is remembered that in international society States are their own law-makers. From the analytical point of view, the binding force of all rules of international law ultimately rests on their consent, recognition, acquiescence or the principle of estoppel. If States consider themselves bound by a given rule as a rule of international law, it is difficult to see why it should not be treated as such in so far as these States are concerned".[39]

There is of course a fundamental difference between voting for a resolution declaring that States are to be guided by certain rules (let alone a resolution declaring that States *should* be guided by certain rules), and considering that one is oneself, already, bound by a certain rule because it is a rule of international law. There is a suspicion of a *petitio principii* in the argument: if it were already the case that resolutions of the General Assembly created rules which were binding as part of general international law, then the act of voting for such a resolution would constitute consent to be bound by such a rule; but one cannot base the conclusion that voting has such an effect on the assumption that it does so. [Thus, if it is argued (for example) that a resolution purporting to declare a rule of international law could be binding on, at the least, the States which voted for it, on the basis of some sort of estoppel, the difficulty immediately encountered is that estoppel only arises if the act by which a State is allegedly estopped created or gave rise to an expectation (relied upon by other States) that that State would act in conformity with it; but such an expectation is only justified once it has become established that a State which has voted for such a resolution is estopped in this way from behaving inconsistently with the resolution.[40] It is in fact necessary to assume the conclusion in order to get the argument on its feet.]

The difficulty of any voluntaristic position with regard to customary law is ultimately that it is hard put to it to explain the

39. Bin Cheng, *op. cit.*, at p. 37; [in the same sense see Lachs, The International Law of Outer Space, 113 *Recueil des Cours,* 1964-III, at p. 98.]

40. [Cf. Bleicher, The Legal Significance of Re-citation of General Assembly Resolutions, 63 A.J.I.L. (1969), 444 at p. 447.]

applicability of general international law to States which have not participated in the custom in the course of its formation, or are not in agreement with it. Thus Dr. Cheng in fact appears to draw back somewhat from his first position, when he classifies the *opinio juris* exemplified in an Assembly resolution, which in his view suffices of itself to create customary law, as *opinio juris communis* as between the member States of the United Nations[41] – or possibly among those which vote for the resolution in question –, as opposed to the *opinio juris generalis* which is creative of rules of customary law binding on the whole international community. Thus the type of customary law which Dr. Cheng would contend can be created by Assembly resolutions is purely local or regional customary law,[42] which binds only those States which have accepted it expressly, by voting for the resolution which states it, or otherwise.

Even to this limited position it may be objected that if immediately binding law can come into operation, even between a limited group of States, merely by virtue of concordant or joint assertions of a rule through the representatives of States at the United Nations or in other international organizations, unaccompanied either by practice applying the rule to the concrete interests of the States concerned, or by the more usual operations by which States express consent to be bound by given rules – ratification of or accession to a treaty containing the rule – it is difficult to see why law-making *treaties* should ever have been thought necessary, or – take the example upon which Dr. Cheng founds his argument – why the 1965 Outer Space Treaty was ever drawn up.

It is clear that the law-making activity which Dr. Cheng regards as within the power of the General Assembly cannot properly be called legislative, any more than it can properly be called the creation of customary law; for the main advantage [if not the distinguishing mark,] of legislative activity is that it enables the majority to create law binding on the minority, which – subject to proper safeguards – becomes necessary in most reasonably advanced societies. It is also doubtful whether, assuming the development postulated by Dr. Cheng to have taken place, it is basically

41. [This appears to have been the position of Judge Tanaka in the *South West Africa* cases, *I.C.J. Reports 1966*, p. 250 at p. 293.]

42. On local custom, see below, p. 136ff.

desirable in the long term. The codification of the law by treaty is a slow process, even though more rapid – in many cases – than custom; but its is less likely to be influenced by political considerations than is the voting in international assemblies, and more likely to involve a studied and deliberate act of choice by each State concerned. Custom on the other hand grows slowly – though not always as slowly as heretofore[43] – but it grows through the actual practice of States, and therefore tends to reflect accurately the balance of their conflicting interests, and to represent their considered intentions. "Instant" custom may have the defects of both systems and the merits of neither.

[From "instant custom", we may turn to a related concept, that of law by "consensus", recently examined in an important article by Professor d'Amato.[44] The contention advanced in this article is that international law by consensus may emerge from General Assembly resolutions, and that such law will be binding on all States which voted for the resolution in question and on States which abstained in the relevant vote, but not on States which voted against the resolution. The central pillars of the argument are first, that consensus is to be distinguished from consent, and secondly that consensus

> "is *not* a law-creating process, even though it is often conveniently referred to as such. Consensus – the inference we draw from the process of international communication about norms – *is* international law; what States *believe* to be law is law."[45]

This thesis will be recognised – although it is not specifically advanced as such – as a means of turning the flank of the principle discussed above,[46] that no new source of law can come into existence except through the operation of one of the existing sources of law. If consensus is a source of law, to be distinguished from consent, in the sense of agreement normally embodied in treaties, and to be distinguished also from the psychological element or *opinio juris* in the creation of customary law,[47] then, if

43. The law of the continental shelf – excluding the alleged "equidistance rule" – has undoubtedly grown since the war, if not in a shorter time. Cf. the observation of Judge Tanaka quoted on p. 2 above, note 4.

44. On Consensus, VIII *Canadian Yearbook of International Law,* 1970, p. 104.

45. *Op. cit.,* p. 121; italics original.

46. See p. 39.

47. Professor d'Amato rejects Dr. Bin Cheng's effective identification of consensus in an international assemby with *opinio juris: op. cit.,* pp. 111-2.

the principle referred to is accepted, consensus must be able to show proofs of descent from one of the traditionally recognised sources of law. But, against this, it is difficult to dispute the claim that "what States believe to be law, is law", at least in the sense that a rule which is universally, or even generally, believed to be part of international law clearly is a rule of international law, however unsatisfactory its ancestry – or for that matter, what is has to say – may be to jurists. If consensus *is* law, the question of the source of the rule enshrined in or endorsed by the consensus appears to fade into the background.

But fade as it may, the question of sources can not be entirely exorcised. It is true that what States believe to be law is law; but it must be supposed that the States in question consider themselves to have grounds for their belief, that is to say, they will believe that the rule in question has become part of international law in some way, that is to say that it has a source. If the consensus is to the effect that the rule has become law through the operation of a recognised source of international law, then consensus as a concept would not appear to add anything to previous thinking on the subject.[48] If on the other hand it is contended that the consensus is to the effect that the rule is law because of the consensus, then consensus is being treated as a source of law, and the problem re-appears of how consensus became a source of law.]

To sum up, in the light of the discussion in this Chapter of the claims of resolutions of international organizations to legislative or law-making effect, it may be as well to stress three points. First, it is submitted that it is clear that it is not possible to create law by custom in areas of human existence and inter-State relations, in which States have not yet penetrated sufficiently for there to be anything more than a sketch of international practice: the obvious example is the "law" governing activities in outer space. In this field, there are many problems – including some of those which the 1963 Declaration and the 1965 Treaty attempt to resolve – which would only be capable of being settled by customary law when the technological skills and techniques which could transfer

48. [At one point, Professor d'Amato seems to be contemplating consensus as operating in this way, when he sums up his position in the significantly different words following: "If all States subscribe to a declaration that a particular formula expresses an existing rule of law, then that is the end of the matter, for what States believe to be international law is *international law common usage*" (italics added); *op. cit.*, at p. 106.]

such problems from the plane of the expected to that of the actual are within the grasp of mankind. Attempts to settle such problems before they arise by means of multilateral treaties are wholly to be commended as wise and prudent, and in harmony with the spirit of the United Nations Charter; but attempts, in this field above all, to make law by novel and doubtful techniques are to be deprecated as liable to create an illusion of security in the law which is likely to be sharply dispelled as soon as any of the declared principles comes into abrupt conflict with State interests.

Secondly, rather similar considerations apply to questions which have always been excluded from the scope and operation of customary law by virtue of a basic rule of customary law, and in particular matters which have always been within the reserved domain of States. This is not to deny that the extent of the reserved domain must vary with the development of international relations:[49] but encroachments on it are more likely to be effectively made by treaty than by declarations purporting to state customary law. It must be emphasised that even though the treatement by States of their own nationals may, with regard to many or most of the States of the world, be consistent with itself and in harmony with that of other States, or most other States: but yet the practice is of no value in the creation of custom, because no obligation of which international law can take cognisance can come into existence between a State and persons who are not subjects of international law.

Finally, attention should be drawn to the dangers inherent in attempting to disguise a sort of legislation by consensus as a class of customary law. It is of course fundamental that a treaty rule, as such, binds only those States which have expressly assented to its application to them, whereas a rule of customary law binds all States of the international community (unless it is a local custom, and with the exception of what Sir Gerald Fitzmaurice has called "recalcitrant States",[50] which have manifested consistent opposition from an early enough moment). Hence to refer to General Assembly resolutions adopted by majority vote – or even by unanimous vote of the members at the time – as imposing *customary* law is bound to lead to repudiation of such "law" sooner or

49. See *Nationality Decrees issues in Tunis and Morocco, P.C.I.J. Series B, No. 4,* p. 24.

50. See 92 *Recueil des Cours,* 1957-II, p. 99.

later; [and if law which purports to be general is repudiated with impunity, its authority is severely shaken.] If it is frankly recognised that changes can only come by free and definite consent, progress will be more sure in the long run.

It may be desirable that there should be an international legislature within or without the United Nations. But it cannot be contended that the Charter itself bound States members to accept such a law-making technique,[51] and since no new source of law can, as we have noted, emerge *ex nihilo,* either amendment of the Charter or developments properly to be regarded as customary law are necessary to bring this about.

The late Judge Alvarez observed in 1951 that

> "... the [General] Assembly of the United Nations is tending to become an actual international legislative power. In order that it may actually become such a power, all that is needed is that Governments and public opinion should give it support".[52]

It is to be feared that there has not yet been the requisite degree of clearly evinced support by Governments, whatever the state of public opinion may be, to produce the result indicated by Judge Alvarez.

51. It will be recalled that the Philippine proposal at the San Francisco conference to give the Assembly legislative powers was overwhelmingly rejected: *U.N.C.I.O. Documents,* Vol. IX, p. 70.

52. Dissenting Opinion, *Reservations to Genocide Convention, I.C.J. Reports 1951,* at p. 53.

Chapter Six

THE INTERACTION OF CUSTOM AND CODIFYING TREATIES

As we have seen, the conclusion of a codifying treaty normally presupposes the existence of at least a fair amount of established customary law in the field to be covered by the treaty; a treaty which breaks entirely new ground can only be termed "codifying" by a rather excessively flexible use of that term. If therefore there is such a basis of customary law for the matter to be "ripe for codification", then it is possible for the conclusion, or even the mere signing, of a codifying treaty to constitute the last item of State practice required for the estabiishment of the rules set out in the treaty, or some of them, as rules of general customary law; the treaty will thus have the effect of "crystallising" the rules in the field concerned which have not, prior to the treaty, quite attained the status of customary law.

This was one of the submissions of the Governments of Denmark and the Netherlands in the Continental Shelf cases with regard to the so-called "equidistance rule" for the delimitation of areas of continental shelf,[1] set out in Article 6 of the 1958 Geneva Convention on the Continental Shelf. The Judgment of the International Court, while conceding that certain provisions of the Convention, in particular the more general provisions declaring the existence of rights of the coastal State over the continental shelf off its coasts, were part of general law, declined to recognise that Article 6 of the Convention represented or had crystallised emerging customary law, on the ground that

1. See paragraphs 61-62 of the Judgment, *I.C.J. Reports 1969*, p. 38. In the discussion of these cases which follows, the question of "special circumstances" as qualifying the alleged general "equidistance rule" has been ignored, for the sake of simplicity, since although it played an important part in the decision of the case, it is not germane to the problems here discussed.

"the principle of equidistance . . . was proposed by the [International Law] Commission with considerable hesitation, somewhat on an experimental basis, at most *de lege ferenda* and not at all *de lege lata* or as an emerging rule of customary international law".[2]

but the Court by no means excluded the possibility that the adoption of a convention, or even of a draft convention, might have the "crystallising" effect claimed for Article 6 of the Geneva Convention on the Continental Shelf.

Another law-making process, possibly of more frequent occurrence, and one which was also discussed in the course of the *Continental Shelf* cases is that whereby the existence of a codifying treaty stimulates the crystallisation of customary rules on the lines laid down, for the parties to the treaty, in the treaty. The process was described by the International Court as follows:

". . . this contention . . . involves treating that Article [sc., Article 6 of the Geneva Convention] as a norm-creating provision which has constituted the foundation of, or has generated a rule which, while only conventional or contractual in its origin, has since passed into the general *corpus* of international law, and is now accepted as such by the *opinio juris*, so as to have become binding even for countries which have never, and do not, become parties to the Convention".

The Court added that

"There is no doubt that this process is a perfectly possible one and does from time to time occur",[3]

and no examples were thought necessary to illustrate the point.[4]

[The "generation" of customary law by treaties has recently been studied by Professor d'Amato,[5] and before proceeding further with this aspect of the *Continental Shelf* case, it may be convenient to take stock of some aspects of this study. Professor d'Amato is at considerable pains to demonstrate that

". . . generalizable provisions in bilateral and multilateral treaties generate customary rules of law binding upon all States";[6]

a statement which may seem unremarkable if it is not observed that it is wholly unqualified – that it does not assert, as the International Court does, that the process is "a possible one" but

2. *I.C.J. Reports 1969*, p. 38, para. 62.

3. *Ibid.*, page 41, para. 71.

4. For examples, see generally R.R. Baxter, Multilateral Treaties as Evidence of International Law, 41 *B.Y.I.L.* (1965-1966) p. 275, at 294ff.

5. *The Concept of Custom in International Law*, Cornell University Press, 1971.

6. *Op. cit.*, p. 104.

that it is an actual and presumably inevitable one. This more extreme view again may seem unexceptionable if all that is meant is that all generalizable provisions in bilateral and multilateral treaties constitute, in the traditional terminology (which Professor d'Amato rejects), acts of State practice and at the same time evidence – of greater or less weight according to circumstances – of the existence of *opinio juris*. This does in fact appear to be what Professor d'Amato is saying in the following passage:

> "The theory underlining[7] the fact that treaties generate customary law is also simple. As we have seen, customary law contains a quantitative element and a qualitative one. With respect to the former, treaties clearly supply the necessary *commitment* to act, as well as, in most cases, subsequent implementation . . . The other component of custom, the qualitative element, is if anything more evident in treaties than in ordinary acts of States".[8]

However, the extent to which Professor d'Amato's views appear to diverge from more traditional theories of the relation of treaties to customary law is demonstrated by his contention as to the time element in the process under consideration. If a treaty is simply equated with one act (or possibly more, in the case of a multilateral treaty) of State practice, and treated also as evidence of *opinio juris* with regard to the States concerned, it is undoubtedly highly *relevant* to any consideration of international customary law in the field to which the treaty relates; but it does not, in the present writer's view at least, necessarily operate to create a rule of customary law binding on all States unless or until the circumstances are such as to indicate the existence of a "*general* practice accepted as law". The conclusion of a bilateral treaty showing an intention to adopt a particular course of action as a matter of law may well in time, if adopted as an example to be followed, or even if merely tacitly approved, "generate" a customary rule; but it would seem to be *a priori* unlikely that it could be accepted from the outset as having generated a rule binding on other States.

Yet this is the view which Professor d'Amato advances. It is not merely that treaties are relevant in the ascertainment of custom; on the contrary

> "The claim made here is . . . that generalizable provisions in treaties give rise to rules of customary law binding upon all States";[9]

7. Possibly a misprint for "underlying"?
8. *Op. cit.*, at p. 160.
9. d'Amato, *op. cit.*, p. 107.

and it is not a question of treaties usually, or even sometimes, generating rules which become binding rules at a later date, by virtue of subsequent developments (or lack of them):

> "If treaties do at any point in time pass into customary law, they pass at the moment they are ratified".[10]

One may ask, in passing, why it should be the moment of ratification which is critical, and not some other moment, for example, more generally the moment of entry into force, which might not be the moment of ratification but that of signature, or the moment of signature, when the text becomes definitive, or again the moment when the treaty becomes public knowledge, e.g., by registration under Article 102 of the UN Charter.

Perhaps the most striking point of Professor d'Amato's argument is the theory of the immediate passage of treaties into customary law, in the sense of creation of rules of customary law binding on all States; and it is this aspect of his argument that does not appear to be supported by the considerable body of evidence – State practice, judicial decisions, opinions of writers – which he cites. The conclusion seems dictated more by theoretical considerations: in Professor d'Amato's view, the greater "persuasiveness" of a treaty ratified ten years ago as against one only a week old is "only a behavioural theory and not a difference in kind", and he rejects the view that "a treaty does become custom at a particular time but no-one can tell when the time comes" because

> "... it would make no sense to say that a treaty has no effect upon customary law for the first four years and six months of its existence, but in the seventh month of the fifth year suddenly becomes transmuted into customary law ... the fact that no-one can specify a time is a strong argument in support of the proposition that there *is no* such dividing line".[11]

So expressed, the problem recalls the old riddle of how many straws make a heap, and the answer surely is the same: the fact that we cannot say precisely how many straws make a heap does not lead us to deny the possible existence of a heap of straw; nor does it oblige us to say that the heap is constituted by the placing of the first straw, – or, for that matter, the last.

However, the truth seems to be that when Professor d'Amato

10. *Ibid.*, p. 164.
11. *Op. cit.*, pp. 163-164.

talks of custom or customary law, he is in fact not talking about the same thing as customary law in the sense used in the present study. As we have already noted,[12] Professor d'Amato's approach is "claim-oriented" and he views customary law as a process rather than as a set of rules. It appears therefore – but the present writer is ready to admit that he is not wholly confident of having fully grasped Professor d'Amato's thought – that all that is meant by the argument quoted is that from the moment of its creation, a treaty begins to exercise a certain pressure upon States non-parties to the treaty, tending to induce them to adapt their conduct to the view of the law contained in or implied by the treaty; and this pressure may in favourable circumstances attain such a point that a tribunal can, *ex post facto*, refer to that view as amounting to a rule of law. For Professor d'Amato, the treaty is part of customary law as soon as it begins to exert pressure; for us, for reasons already explained,[13] it seems more useful to speak of the treaty as legally relevant forthwith, but as only entering customary law, or generating a rule of customary law, when the "rule" is no longer merely persuasive but absolute. If the above is a correct understanding of Professor d'Amato's argument, the debate is really one of terminology.

We may therefore now return to our examination of the *North Sea Continental Shelf* cases, in which] the Court proceeded to an illuminating examination of the conditions which must be satisfied for the process which has been referred to as "generation" of a customary rule by a treaty to be regarded as having taken place with regard to a particular provision in a treaty, which is alleged to have passed into general international law. The provision in question must be

> "at all events potentially . . . of a fundamentally norm-creating character",[14]

that is to say, it must be of such a kind that it can operate as a general rule. In this connection attention was drawn to the fact that in the case of the 1958 Geneva Convention on the Continental Shelf, it was permissible to make reservations to (inter alia) Article 6; and the Court observed on this point that this possibility

> "while it might not of itself prevent the equidistance principle being eventually

12. See above, pp. 50-51.
13. [See above, p. 51.]
14. *I.C.J. Reports 1969*, p. 42, para. 72.

> received as general law, does add considerably to the difficulty of regarding this result as having been brought about . . . on the basis of the Convention".[15]

The whole question of reservations to codifying, or purportedly codifying, treaties is a difficult one, to which we shall have to return.[16]

Clearly the State practice which would convert the treaty-rule into a rule of customary law would normally consist of acts by States in the normal course of their international relations, harmonising with the rules laid down in the treaty; in the particular field of the law of the continental shelf, this would be actual delimitations of continental shelf areas on the lines laid down in the 1958 Geneva Convention. But it appears that this category of acts may be at once too wide and too narrow: on the one hand, it was argued for Denmark and the Netherlands that ratifications of the Convention could themselves be taken into account in weighing up the practice of States since the date of the Convention; and on the other hand, the question was raised of the value as precedents to be taken into account in this connection of delimitations of continental shelf areas by States parties to the 1958 Convention.

On the first point, the essential distinction, to which attention has already been drawn, is between acts which constitute State practice (and may at the same time afford evidence of the existence of the *opinio juris*) and acts by States which, while possibly affording evidence of their views as to the legal status of given rules, do not amount to acts of State practice which may be taken into account when considering the question of the existence of a rule of customary law. On which side of this line does the act of ratifying a general codifying treaty fall? This is a question we have already touched on,[17] but it is worth considering more closely, in the form it took in the *North Sea Continental Shelf* cases.

The argument of the Respondents (Denmark and the Netherlands) was clearly expressed in their pleadings. In the Danish Reply, the following statement:

> "If the acceptances[18] of the Convention by States since 1958 testify, by their

15. *Ibid.*
16. See below, p. 118ff.
17. See above, pp. 67-8.
18. Explained as covering "ratifications, accessions and 'notifications of succession' " (I.C.J. *Pleadings, Oral Arguments, Documents,* Vol. I, p. 190, note).

> number and character, to the general recognition by the international community of Article 6 [of the Convention] as expressing the rules of international law, so also does the practice of States in *applying* the Convention"[19]

appears in the Section of the pleading entitled "The State Practice since the Geneva Conference of 1958". Again, in the Common Rejoinder of Denmark and the Netherlands, it is asserted that

> "State practice since the Geneva Conference, by the numerous ratifications of the Geneva Convention and by the numerous delimitations of continental shelf boundaries on the basis of the principles expressed in Article 6, amply confirms that today those principles possess the status of the generally recognized rules of international law . . ."[20]

Since the Court held that Article 6 of the Convention had not in fact become a rule of general international law, inter alia because the amount of State practice shown to exist was insufficient, it was essential for it to rule on the value of ratifications of the Convention as State practice, which it did in the following words:

> "With respect to the other elements usually regarded as necessary before a conventional rule can be considered to have become a general rule of international law, it might be that . . . a very widespread and representative participation in the convention might suffice of itself, provided it included that of States whose interests were specially affected".[21]

The extremely guarded form of expression adopted will be noted; since the Court was deciding that Article 6 of the Convention of 1958 was *not* general international law, it was bound to be cautious as to what practice would be required to make such a treaty-provision into general law,[22] the more so, in that the Court was also of the view that Article 6 was probably not suitable in its expression to be adopted as general international law. Nonetheless, the passage just quoted clearly indicates that, with all necessary reservations, the view of the Court was that in appropriate cases "widespread and representative" participation in a Convention may suffice both as evidence of *opinio juris* and as sufficient State practice.

At the same time, it must be borne in mind that any assessment of the significance of a ratification of a codifying treaty must be a

19. *Pleadings, Oral Arguments, Documents*, Vol. I, p. 192.
20. *Ibid.*, p. 478.
21. *I.C.J. Reports 1969* p. 43, para. 73.
22. Cf. Lauterpacht, *The Development of International Law by the International Court*, pp. 75ff.

cautious one, as must any assessment also be of abstentions from ratification.[23]

This view gives rise to two difficulties, which however will be found on examination to be more apparent than real. The first results from the equating of ratifications with State practice in the traditional sense: we have already emphasised the need for the "material element" in the formation of custom to be "concrete" in the sense of having direct practical effect,[24] so as to exclude from the category of acts contributing to the formation of custom mere declarations *in abstracto*. The second difficulty is also one on which we have already touched,[25] and relates to the nature of the *opinio juris* in the particular case of the ratification of a general convention as an act of State practice.

An objection to the view adopted by the Court based on the first of these two points would, it would seem, be on safe ground insofar as it emphasised that ratifications of a treaty setting out certain general rules to be applied in the future, while it is evidence of the desire of the ratifying State to accept those rules, and possibly of the view of the ratifying State that those rules are in accordance with existing law, would not on a traditional view of the matter have been regarded as an *act* of State practice, as would the ratification of a treaty actually giving practical effect to those rules, i.e., in this particular field, a treaty effecting an agreed delimitation of continental shelf areas in a given locality. As has already been suggested above, however, the Court's view of the matter is surely sound, particularly when read in context: as we shall see, the inclusion of ratifications of a general treaty in the category of State practice involves the exclusion of more concrete acts by the ratifying States; and even if a State which has ratified the treaty does not in fact ever apply it, ratification differs radically from a mere assertion of rules in the abstract, even coupled with a statement that those rules are accepted by the State concerned, since ratification involves direct and immediate acceptance of them as binding, and commonly permanently binding, on the State concerned.

The second difficulty is that if the traditional and narrow interpretation of *opinio juris* is adopted, namely the requirement

23. See para. 73 of the *Continental Shelf* Judgment, foot of p. 42.
24. See above, p. 68.
25. See above, p. 67.

that the relevant acts of States were carried out in the belief that the State concerned was required so to act by an international custom amounting to a rule of law, then the equating of ratification of a codifying treaty with an "act" contributing to State practice leads to a curious result. To take the particular example of the equidistance principle in Article 6 of the Geneva Convention, if there existed, at any given moment after the conclusion of the Convention, a rule of general customary law requiring the delimitation of continental shelf areas to be effected on the basis of equidistance, then all States were bound so to delimit their continental shelves; but it surely cannot be argued that they were bound, by the same rule of customary law, to ratify the treaty. In a sense, if such a rule requiring delimitation on the basis of equidistance had passed into general international law, there would have been all the less reason to ratify the treaty, since it had served its purpose, and could add nothing more to the legal situation.

This is equally the case if, following the suggestion of Mr. MacGibbon,[26] we assert that *opinio juris* is only to be looked for on the part of those States whose position with regard to each individual act of State practice considered is the passive one – i.e. States which make no objection to a claim must, if their abstention is to be taken as significant, have done so because they considered that the claim was justified in law; but it is irrelevant that the claimant State may, and probably will, have made its claim for reasons of convenience or interest, without regard to whether it is required by, or even in accordance with, the law. This theory cannot be reconciled with the International Court's view that ratifications are acts of State practice, for the act of ratifying a treaty is a purely unilateral act, which may be effected by any State to which the treaty was open, and which it cannot be open to any other State to comment on, let alone protest against;[27] thus, on Mr. MacGibbon's theory, no *opinio juris* would exist on either "side" in the case of the ratification of a treaty.

The difficulty of reconciling the Court's view with the tradi-

26. Customary Law and Acquiescence, 33 *B.Y.I.L.* (1957) p. 115ff. See above, p. 48.

27. Unless, of course, subject to reservations unacceptable to another State party to the treaty. (Only general "law-making" treaties are being considered here, not bilateral treaties which may affect the rights of other States.)

tional interpretation of the *opinio juris* was apparently recognised by Judge Lachs, who dissented from the majority of the Court in the *North Sea Continental Shelf* cases in holding that the "equidistance rule" had passed into general international law. His standpoint on the meaning of *opinio juris* was as follows:

> "... it is surely over-exacting to require proof that every State having applied a given rule did so because it was conscious of an *obligation* to do so. What can be required is that the party relying on an alleged general rule must prove that the rule invoked is part of a general practice accepted as law by the States in question".[28]

The meaning of "the States in question" in the second sentence is not entirely clear, but it is evident from the first sentence that in any event Judge Lachs would not require a State ratifying the Geneva Convention to have done so because it felt that it was bound by law to do so, for its ratification to be included in the category of State practice leading to the formation of customary law.[29]

It is however suggested that it is also possible to regard ratifications of a general convention as acts of State practice accompanied by *opinio juris* if the latter term is widened, as suggested earlier,[30] to include the intention to conform to, and assist the emergence of, a developing rule of customary law. The matter is not one of obligation, since by definition if the rule has not yet crystallised as part of general international law it cannot require that States conform their actions to it. At the stage of development of the rule now under consideration, what is needed is the recognition of the rule as a desirable one, and not a matter of mere courtesy or convenience, accompanying any act designed to further its entry into general customary law. Such an act may be simply adoption of the rule to guide the effective actions of the State concerned in the field in question; or it may equally well be the act of lending the support of the State to a codifying treaty designed to bring the rule into effective play in the whole international community.

There remains the other question raised by the *North Sea Continental Shelf* cases with regard to State practice, namely what is the relevance of acts which would normally constitute evidence

28. *I.C.J. Reports 1969*, p. 231.

29. Earlier in his Opinion, Judge Lachs surveys in detail the ratifications of the Geneva Convention as elements of State practice: pp. 225-229.

30. See above, pp. 53-54.

of State practice – namely, in the particular case, acts of delimitation of continental shelf areas – if they are effected by States which are, or which shortly thereafter become, parties to a general convention providing for such acts to be carried out?

If the act of ratification of a treaty, which has little direct and immediately practical content, can be regarded as a relevant act of State practice, one would expect, *prima facie,* acts of States parties to the Convention in question, either after ratification or prior to ratification, to have carried still more force as contributing to the establishment of a rule of general law. But in the *Continental Shelf* cases, the Court began its examination of the evidence of acts of delimitation of continental shelf areas since 1958 as follows:

> "... over half the States concerned, whether acting unilaterally or conjointly, were or shortly became parties to the Geneva Convention and were therefore presumably, so far as they were concerned, acting actually or potentially in the application of the Convention. From their action no inference could legitimately be drawn as to the existence of a rule of customary international law ...".[31]

At first sight, this argument seems to produce a very curious result. If a rule is contained in a multilateral treaty which is such as to be capable of being applied as a rule of customary international law, and numerous States become parties to the treaty, there would appear to be a danger that the transition of the rule from treaty-law status to that of customary law will be indefinitely delayed or prevented. After becoming a party to the treaty, each State will, when applying the rule in question, merely be doing so because the treaty requires it to do so, and not because of the presence of any *opinio juris*, for the State in question cannot be presumed to have been acting as it did because it considered a rule of *customary law* bound it to do so.[32] Thus each State which becomes a party to the treaty withdraws itself from the body of States which can contribute, by suitable acts, to the formation of customary law on the matter covered by the treaty; and this

31. *I.C.J. Reports 1969,* p. 44, para. 76.

32. [It was contended by Denmark and the Netherlands in the *Continental Shelf* cases that such an act would be "fully relevant, even if it may do little more than confirm an *opinio juris* on the part of [the States concerned] which was already implicit in their previous ratifications of the ... Convention" (*I.C.J. Pleadings, Oral Arguments, Documents*, Vol. I, p. 491); but the fact that a State does an act which it is, in the circumstances, required to do by a Convention to which it is a party throws no light whatever on the reasons which induced it to become a party.]

process may result in all States belonging to two camps, those who have so disbarred themselves from contributing to State practice by ratifying the treaty, and those which are uninterested, and which therefore neither ratify the treaty nor act in the matter in any way capable of contributing to the growth of a rule.[33] Thus the material element required for the formation of custom would be, and would continue to be, impossible to create.

However, the argument is in fact really the reverse of the medal, the obverse of which is the view taken by the International Court that ratifications of a treaty of the kind being considered are themselves acts of State practice capable of being counted in the assessment of the material element in the formation of a customary rule. Evidence of State practice must have a certain quantitative content: a certain mathematical element of repetition and frequency is required.[34] In assessing the *generality* of a custom, it is obviously improper to count any State twice, as it were, once when it ratifies a general treaty, and once for each act carried out subsequently in conformity with the rules laid down in the treaty.[35] Successive acts of the same State are only relevant in an examination of the status of an alleged customary rule as showing *consistency* of State practice – which goes to the content of the rule alleged, rather than to its existence – and as indicating the presence also of the psychological element, in that repetition suggests that the State concerned regarded itself as bound to act as it did. But the existence of the general treaty meets both these needs: the content of the rule is fixed in advance, and the only question is *whether* it exists as a customary rule so as to bind non-parties to the treaty. Furthermore, not merely is it impossible to determine *ab extra* whether the State concerned, when it acted in application of a treaty-rule, did or did not believe that it would have been bound to act as it did regardless of the treaty, as a matter of customary law, but also, if ratification may prove *opinio juris* with regard to the ratifying State, any further evidence of *opinio juris* as regards that State is wholly superfluous.

33. [The same conclusion is drawn by Professor Baxter in his 1970 Hague lectures: 129 *Recueil des Cours,* 1970-I, at p. 64.]

34. Sørensen suggests that "Ce qu'il faut exiger, c'est d'une manière générale que la même conduite ait été observée chaque fois que l'occasion s'en est présentée". See *Les sources du droit international*, p. 102; 101 *Recueil des Cours*, 1960-III, p. 40.

35. [In this sense, see Separate Opinion of Judge Ammoun, *North Sea Continental Shelf* cases, *I.C.J. Reports 1969*, p. 128, para. 29.]

[It should be recalled that the International Court of Justice had already in effect held in 1952 that practice in conformity with a treaty cannot be relied on as proof of the development of a custom or usage which may be asserted separately from, and after termination of, the treaty in question. In the case concerning the *Rights of U.S. Nationals in Morocco*, the United States enjoyed rights of consular jurisdiction in Morocco by virtue of the most-favoured-nation clause in a treaty of 1836, which operated to give the United States the benefit of (*inter alia*) the rights conferred on Great Britain by a treaty of 1856. When Great Britain gave up these rights in 1937, one of the arguments advanced by the United States in support of its claim to continue to exercise consular jurisdiction in Morocco was that its rights to do so were founded upon "custom and usage". Thus the United States was in effect asserting and relying upon the principle expressed in Article 43 of the Vienna Convention on the Law of Treaties that

> "The . . . termination . . . of a treaty . . . shall not in any way impair the duty of any State to fulfil any obligation embodied in the treaty to which it would be subject under international law independently of the treaty."

The Court did not comment on the principle, but rejected the argument on the facts, for two reasons: the first was simply that the existence of such customary rights had not been proved, because

> ". . . there has not been sufficient evidence to enable the Court to reach a conclusion that a right to exercise consular jurisdiction founded upon custom or usage has been established in such a manner that it has become binding on Morocco".[36]

The second, and more fundamental reason (which the Court in fact gave first) was that

> ". . . throughout this whole period, the United States consular jurisdiction was in fact based, not on custom or usage, but on treaty rights. At all stages, it was based on the provisions either of the Treaty of 1787 or of the Treaty of 1836, together with the provisions of treaties concluded by Morocco with other Powers, . . . invoked by virtue of the most-favoured-nation clauses".[37]

The case for the United States was considerably strengthened by the fact that it was able to point to the existence of examples of the exercise of consular jurisdiction in Morocco by States which

36. *I.C.J. Reports 1952*, p. 176, at p. 200.
37. *Ibid.*, at p. 199.

enjoyed no treaty rights, and to argue that there therefore existed in Morocco a custom or usage of the exercise by foreign Powers of consular jurisdiction over their respective nationals. The Court nonetheless concluded that

> "This is not enough to establish that the States exercising consular jurisdiction in pursuance of treaty rights enjoyed in addition an independent title thereto based on custom or usage".[38]

It must be emphasized that the custom in question in the *U.S. Nationals in Morocco* case was a special or local custom.[39] In such a case, it is in fact difficult to see how a State in the position of enjoying rights conferred by treaty which are subsequently conferred on, and thereafter contemporaneously enjoyed by, other States by virtue of custom can succeed in maintaining that it has itself also become entitled to customary legal rights.[40] If however the participation in the practice in question is so widespread as to justify the conclusion that a general custom has entered universal international law, it would not seem possible to exclude from its ambit a State which has, as it were, pioneered the practice but has done so and continued to do so under the auspices of a specific treaty.

The particular nature of the problem in the *U.S. Nationals in Morocco* case resulted from the indirect way in which the rights claimed under the 1836 Treaty came to an end. If the United Staes had terminated or denounced the Treaty, it would presumably have done so because it no longer intended to exercise its rights of consular jurisdiction, or was prepared to abandon them in the framework of some wider alteration in its position vis-à-vis Morocco. It is unrealistic to suppose that a State would put an end to a treaty relationship on the ground that the advantages secured to it by the treaty had become part of customary international law, so that the Treaty was *functus officio*[41]: *a fortiori* in the case

38. *I.C.J. Reports 1952*, p. 176, at p. 200.

39. On local custom, see below, pp. 136ff.

40. *Aliter* if the custom has already become established prior to the treaty. Dr. Shihata (The Treaty as a Law-Declaring and Custom-Making Instrument, 22 *Revue égyptienne de droit international* (1966) at pp. 66-7) appears to have misunderstood the Court's Judgment on this point, since it did not find the incorporation of a *prior* usage in the Treaty.

41. O'Connell observes that there are cases of successor States declaring their succession to instruments such as the Declaration of Paris, despite the fact that the principles of the Declaration are undoubtedly now part of customary international law: see Independence and Succession to Treaties, *38 B.Y.I.L.* 1962, at p. 134.

of a general "law-making" treaty.

It has in fact been pointed out[42] that provisions for denunciation in a *soi-disant* declaratory treaty operate, like provisions for reservations, to cast grave doubts on the status of the rules laid down by the treaty as pre-existent rules of customary law.[43] One is here on stronger ground than with regard to the permissibility of reservations: while, as we have noted, reservations may signify non-recognition of an allegedly customary rule, they may also amount only to an invitation to conclude a special régime with the reserving State; but provision for denunciation implies that a State which has accepted the rules of the treaty vis-à-vis all the other parties may subsequently claim to detach itself *unilaterally* from the recognised system. Even if for some reason a State party to such a treaty desires to conclude a special arrangement (not contrary to a rule of *jus cogens* or amounting to a denial of a legal concept), it may do so by special treaty without withdrawing from the multilateral general treaty, since the general treaty will, as between the parties to the subsequent special treaty, apply

> "... only to the extent that its provisions are compatible with those of the later treaty".[44]]

42. By Baxter, in 129 *Recueil des Cours*, 1970-I, at p. 63-64.

43. The Geneva Convention on the Continental Shelf provides for revision but not for denunciation.

44. Vienna Convention on the Law of Treaties, Art. 30, paras. 3 and 4.

Chapter Seven

CUSTOM AS LAW ANCILLARY TO CODIFIED LAW

It is evident that in any branch of international law which has been the subject of a successful exercise in codification – successful in the sense that the codifying instrument has been accepted by a sufficient number of States for it to have acquired a dominating position among sources of law on the question – the role of custom will, apart from the possibility of its taking over and adopting the codified rules, be reduced so as to become a subordinate one. Any treaty, including a multilateral treaty purporting to codify general rules of law, ranks as *lex specialis* which will be the first source looked to for the law on the question as between the parties to a difference; and thus custom is bound to become in a sense merely a supplementary source of law.

It may therefore be convenient, in order to examine the various ways in which customary law may be expected to operate in relation to the rules of codified law, to adopt as a working classification one often applied to equity, which has also come to be generally regarded as a supplementary source of law.[1] Equity has not infrequently been classified, from the point of view of its operation with regard to general law, as equity *secundum legem*, equity *praeter legem*, and equity *contra legem*, that is to say, respectively, equity applied by virtue of the law itself, equity operating alongside the law "in order to remedy its insufficiencies and fill in its logical lacunae",[2] and equity operating in opposition to the law, so as to alter it, or temper its effects in particular cases.[3] Without dwelling on these distinctions, or seeking to draw

1. Cf. *North Sea Continental Shelf* case, Judgment, para. 88 et seqq., *I.C.J. Reports 1969*, p. 48ff.

2. Separate Opinion of Judge Ammoun, ibid., p. 139.

3. It is unfortunate that the writers who use the Latin terms to distinguish the various operations of equity do not agree on their meaning: cf. Bin Cheng in *Current Legal Problems*, 1955, p. 185; Jenks, *The Prospects of International Adjudication*, pp.

too close an analogy between the role of equity in international law and that which we are postulating for international custom in certain fields of international law, we may adopt the convenient shorthand of the Latin labels; but if so, we must first explain what they are each intended to denote.

Custom operating *secundum legem,* or more precisely *secundum legem scriptam,* since custom is of course itself a source of law, even when relegated to a subsidiary position,[4] indicates, in the classification here proposed, custom which applies to govern legal relationships, rights or obligations in a branch of law governed by a treaty, in particular a codifying treaty, by virtue of express or implied provision in the treaty itself to that effect.[5] It may well be the case that certain details of a legal transaction or relationship are not suitable for general, but precise, formulation in a treaty, and are best left to be resolved according to the usual custom of the States concerned; and it will normally be the case that custom which, for some or all of the States parties to the treaty, goes beyond the treaty and does not run counter to it, should be preserved.[6]

An example of this comparatively rare operation of custom in relation to a codifying treaty is afforded by the Convention relating to the Conflict of Nationality Laws, drawn up at The Hague Codification Conference of 1930, which provided in Article 1 that the law enacted by a State for the purpose of determining its nationals

> "shall be recognised by other States insofar as it is consistent with . . . international custom and the principles of law generally recognized with regard to nationality".[7]

Two further, more recent examples may be found in the Vienna Convention on Diplomatic Relations of 18 April 1961. Article 16

316ff.; the Separate Opinions of Judge Ammoun in *I.C.J. Reports 1969,* p. 100 at p. 139 and *I.C.J. Reports 1970,* p. 286 at pp. 332-3; [and V.D. Degan, *L'Equité et le Droit International,* pp. 25ff.]

4. One cannot distinguish between custom and law as one can between law and equity.

5. [This is in fact the approach of the Italian Civil Code to custom: see Article 8 of the Code, quoted in footnote 20 on p. 101 below. A considerable number of Articles of the Italian Code do in fact contain a *renvoi* to customary rules or usages.]

6. Cf. Preamble to Vienna Convention on the Law of Treaties, para. 8.

7. League of Nations Treaty Series, No. 4137, Vol. CLXXIX, p. 90 at p. 99; quoted by the International Court in *Nottebohm (Second Phase) I.C.J. Reports 1955,* p. 23.

of that Convention, which governs precedence as between Heads of Mission, provides in paragraph 3 that the Article

> "is without prejudice to any practice accepted by the receiving State regarding the precedence of the representative of the Holy See".[8]

In other words, the position of the representative of the Holy See is, by virtue of an express provision in the treaty, regulated according to the custom accepted by the receiving State concerned.[9] Similarly, Article 38 of the same Convention, which deals with the immunity of diplomatic agents from jurisdiction, is prefaced by the words

> "Except in so far as additional privileges and immunities may be granted by the receiving State . . ."

Such additional privileges and immunities may of course be granted *ex gratia,* in such a way as not to give rise to a binding custom; but if they are binding as part of local customary law, then as between States parties to the Vienna Convention they will operate by virtue of the Convention, as a result of a sort of *renvoi* to customary law.

Examples of custom secundum legem as here defined are perhaps not likely to be met with frequently,[10] but the category is mentioned for completeness, and because it is one likely to be overlooked. A rather special example which should also be mentioned is the provision in the Vienna Convention on the Law of Treaties for the operation of *jus cogens* (see Articles 53 and 64 of the Convention). The question of whether a treaty conflicts with "a peremptory norm of general international law" is one which can only be dealt with by ascertaining whether the alleged norm does form part of "general international law", i.e. customary law, and if so, what its content is.

Of far more practical importance is the category which we propose to call custom *praeter legem,*[11] that is to say, customary

8. U.N. Treaty Series, Vol. 500.

9. If the question is whether the custom regarding the Vatican envoy is a legally binding one, it may be argued that as between parties to the Convention, Article 16 may have made it so.

10. The original draft Convention on Consular Intercourse and Immunities prepared for the I.L.C. by Professor Zourek contained an excellen example, which did not survive into the final text: see the original draft of Article 13 (defining consular functions), first version, in *I.L.C. Yearbook 1957* Vol. II, p. 91.

11. The role of custom as a "source formelle du droit international positif . . . à coté de la loi juridique en tant que norme *praeter legem* mais non *contra legem*" was

law operating alongside the codified rules, and filling in the inevitable gaps which, if they were not realised and intended at the time when the treaty was concluded, are bound to emerge in the course of the application of the treaty to the manifold circumstances of international relations.

Finally, custom *contra legem* is the term which will be used here to designate the legal rules, principally those which have come into existence since the conclusion of the treaty which is in question in any particular instance, which conflict with the rules laid down in the treaty. This particular aspect of custom as a subsidiary source of law is principally of interest as regards the position of dissentient States, and the development of the law after and beyond the conclusion of the codifying treaty.

Both these two categories will require rather fuller treatement than the comparatively limited concept of custom *secundum legem*.

The first question in which the concept of custom *praeter legem* will have a part to play is that of the interpretation of the codifying treaty governing the question actually in issue. A codyfying treaty, however carefully and precisely drawn, will be just as much in need of interpretation in order to be applied to actual cases as any other treaty; in fact cruces of interpretation are the more likely to arise with regard to a multilateral codifying treaty, first because it will fall to be applied to a greater number of widely differing situations between a greater number of States than an ordinary bilateral or plurilateral *Vertrag,* and secondly because any attempt to lay down general rules in precise terms is practically bound to multiply the number of instances in which it is difficult to fit the rule to the case;[12] this is the experience of all municipal legislatures, and all municipal tribunals called upon to apply the fruits of the legislator's labours. As Oppenheim observed,

> "... it is not at all a fact that codification does away with controversies altogether. Codification certainly clears up many questions of law which have been hitherto debatable, but it creates at the same time new controversies".

Even more pertinent is the same author's observation that

---

discussed, with reference to the allegedly codifying Havana Convention of 1928 in the Colombian Reply in the *Asylum* case: see *I.C.J. Pleadings, Oral Arguments, Documents* in that case, Vol. I, p. 326, and below, p. 100.

12. This is in fact the whole justification for admitting equity as a source of law; on the point, see for example the separate opinion of Sir Gerald Fitzmaurice in the *Barcelona Traction* case, *I.C.J. Reports 1970,* p. 64, at pp. 84-86.

"... together with codification there frequently enters into courts of justice, and into the area of juridical literature, a hair-splitting tendency, and an interpretation of the law which often clings more to the letter and the word of the law than to its spirit and principles".[13]

An immediate problem which must not be overlooked is that of determining whether a multilateral "codifying" treaty – in the sense in which we have been using the term – was in fact intended to be declaratory of the then existing law, and accepted as such by the States parties to it. This question will of course only arise if at least one party to a dispute is not a party to the treaty, and claims that the treaty is not declaratory of customary law. The problem has recently been examined by Professor Baxter, who suggests that the appropriate course

"would be to give presumptive effect as evidence of customary law to the treaty purporting to declare that law while allowing the State or individual against whom the treaty is proffered the right to demonstrate that the particular treaty provision invoked does not correctly express the law".[14]

In the Continental Shelf cases, decided since Professor Baxter wrote these lines, the International Court did not have to fall back on any presumption of this kind, since it was satisfied, largely from the *travaux préparatoires* of the 1958 Geneva Convention, that Article 6 of that Convention had been proposed by the International Law Commission

"with considerable hesitation, somewhat on an experimental basis, at most *de lege ferenda* and not at all *de lege lata* . . .".[15]

It is suggested that examination of the discussions and drafts leading up to the conclusion of such a treaty will in fact usually make it reasonably clear to what extent the treaty was declaratory of existing law and to what extent it was to make new law; such an investigation will also unmask another danger to which Professor Baxter draws attention, namely that of the draftsman who attempts to disguise a change in the law as a mere expression of existing law.[16] However, borderline cases in which an examination of the records gives no assistance will probably occur from time to time, and in such a case the course suggested by Professor Baxter

13. Oppenheim, *International Law* (5th Edition by Lauterpacht), Vol. I, p. 59.

14. Multilateral Treaties as Evidence of Customary International Law, 41 *B.Y.I.L.* (1965-66), p. 275, at p. 290.

15. *I.C.J. Reports 1969,* p. 38, para. 62.

16. *Op. cit.* (see note 14).

is, it is submitted, an appropriate one.

If it is shown, or presumed, that a particular codifying treaty has repeated in systematic form the law existing at the time, a theoretical problems remains, this time as regards the relationships of those States which have ratified the treaty, namely, what becomes of the pre-existing customary law, as between the parties, once the treaty rules have come into operation to take their place? The question may seem a purely academic one. As between the States parties to the treaty, from the time when they become parties and for so long as they remain parties, the rules laid down in the treaty govern their relationships, as *lex specialis* in priority to any customary rules in the field. Whether the treaty is regarded as a formal source of law, or merely as evidence of law, or as source of obligation,[17] it is clear that an *obligation d'ordre conventionnel* exists, so that whether there is also, between the same parties, an *obligation de droit coutumier* may seem a question without practical interest.

Yet this question was raised on the pleadings as a practical issue in the *Asylum* case; it was claimed in the Peruvian Government's Counter-Memorial that

> "On ne peut plus parler (en admettant qu'on l'ait jamais pu) de droit coutumier de l'asile interne aux Etats-Unis, ni en Amérique latine, *parce que la matière a été codifiée, et que le droit consuétudinaire, même s'il avait existé, aurait fait place dès lors au droit conventionnel*"[18] (italics original)

The Counter-Memorial continued with the following remarkable statement:

> "C'est un phénomène juridique constant que la codification abroge les coutumes, et cela non seulement en droit interne, mais en droit international".[18]

The weakness of this argument is of course that it takes a phenomenon of municipal law, translates it on to the plane of international law, and asserts that the same phenomenon – or rather the parallel phenomenon to which the same name is applied – produces the same results. Even admitting that in municipal legal systems, codification abrogates custom, which is in any event doubtful,[19] the wholly different nature of codification

17. See above, p. 26.

18. *I.C.J., Asylum, Pleadings, Oral Arguments, Documents,* Vol. I, p. 131.

19. On the introduction of the Code civil in France, the Law of 30 Ventôse Year XII specifically enacted, in Article 7, that general and local customs were thereby abrogated. Nevertheless, "en fait, les coutumes de l'ancienne France ont subsisté dans les interstices du Code civil" (Carbonnier, *Droit Civil,* Vol. I, p. 106, who gives examples of this).

by treaty (or generally accepted declaration) requires at the least a very cautious approach to the hypothesis that codification of the latter kind abrogates international customary law. The first step must clearly be to establish the intentions of the authors [of the municipal code,[20] or] of the codifying treaty; and it is curious that in the *Asylum* case, the Colombian Reply prefers, instead of adopting the standpoint just mentioned, to meet the argument on its own ground, that of the assertion of the essential identity of the concepts dignified, in municipal and in international law, with the name of codification.[21]

In any event, the argument between the parties in this case, taken in isolation, is rather misleading as to the essential point at issue. The Havana Convention of 1928 had, it was agreed, to some extent codified the regional customary law of Latin America on diplomatic asylum, although it was disputed how much customary law had in fact existed prior to the conclusion of the Convention. But Colombia was seeking to assert a right – that of unilateral qualification of the offence committed by the fugitive as political or non-political, by the diplomatic representative giving asylum – which was not referred to in the Havana Convention, but which was asserted by Colombia to have been a right recognised by regional customary law both before and after the conclusion of the Convention of 1928. Thus what the Peruvian Government was really arguing in its Counter-Memorial was that codification in a particular field abrogates all the customary rules in that field; that codification must be taken to be complete and exhaustive, so that an alleged customary rule which, if it existed, might have been expected to have been included in the codifying document will, if

20. [For example, see the limited formula of the Einführungsgesetz zum Bürgerlichen Gesetzbuche, Art. 32: "Die Vorschriften der Reichsgesetze [defined in Art. 2 as "jede Rechtsnorm"] . . . treten jedoch insoweit ausser Kraft, als sich aus dem Bürgerlichen Gesetzbuch oder aus diesem Gesetze die Aufhebung ergibt"; the Netherlands Law of 16 May 1829 (Stb. No. 33), Art. 1: "Insgelijks zijn . . . afgeschaft de algemeene en plaatselijke gebruiken in de stoffen welke bij het nieuwe wetboek worden behandeld". The Spanish Civil Code is more radical in its exclusion of custom; see Art. 1976: "Quedan derogados todos los Cuerpos legales, usos y costumbres que constituyen el Derecho civil común en todas las materias que son objeto de este Código, y quedarán sin fuerza y vigor, así en su concepto de Leyes directamente obligatorias, como en el de derecho supletorio . . .". The Italian Civil Code provides for the application of custom only where the Code contains a *renvoi* to custom (custom *secundum legem*): see Art. 8: "Nelle materie regolate dalle leggi e dai regolamenti gli usi hanno efficacia solo in quanto sono da essi richiamati"; for examples, see ibid., arts. 896, 1181 et seqq. etc.]

21. See *I.C.J. Pleadings, Oral Arguments, Documents* in the case, Vol. I, p. 329.

it does not in fact appear specifically in the text, be taken either never to have existed as a customary rule, or to have been done away with from the date of entry into force of the codifying instrument.

One might assert in answer to this that, once again, the matter must depend on the intentions of the parties to the Convention in question; but even if the rule advanced by Peru were no more than a presumption applicable in the absence of evidence either that the parties intended to preserve, or that they intended to abrogate, customary rules not referred to in a codifying convention, the effects might be far-reaching. The International Court did not have to resolve the point, since it found that the existence of the custom which Colombia claimed to be able to rely on had not in fact been proved (whether prior to the Havana Convention or subsequently);[22] but it is suggested that the arguments of the Colombian Reply are to be preferred on the point.

The latter pleading points out that

> "une concordance absolue entre les traités et les faits est en elle-même irréalisable",[23]

and concludes that

> "Il y aura toujours place pour une révélation du droit au moyen de la coutume,[24] qui demeure . . . non seulement une des sources formelles de l'ordre juridique international, mais le support de toute jurisprudence positive . . .
> . . . les traités internationaux seraient dépourvus de sens et resteraient sans effet si la coutume *praeter legem* ne venait pas à l'appui de l'interprétation exégétique du texte pour autoriser les décisions de la jurisprudence".[25]

One cannot but agree that it must be possible, in order to interpret a convention, and in particular a codifying convention, to refer to the antecedent (if in the particular instance that term does not beg the question) customary law. The question is again one of presumptions, although the Colombian Reply, in the section just quoted, does not make any mention of the question of the intention of the parties as such; what is asserted is that the codifying convention, in the absence of any contrary indication, is to be read as having taken over and re-enacted the customary rules *tels quels*, so that lack of mention of a subsidiary aspect of a

22. See *I.C.J. Reports 1950*, at p. 277.
23. *Pleadings*, Vol. I, p. 327.
24. The natural-law approach implied in these words will be observed!
25. *Pleadings*, Vol. I, pp. 327-8 and p. 329.

custom does not mean, again in the absence of evidence of an intention to exclude, that from the time of the convention onwards the customary rule is to operate shorn of that particular detail.

Whether this is the same as saying that the custom, as a custom, continues to exist alongside the treaty-regime is more doubtful. It really depends on whether one regards the incidental right claimed as having been "adopted" by the treaty, so that it too becomes a *droit conventionnel,* although an implied one; or whether since, as the Colombian Reply observes, no treaty can cover every aspect of the manifold situations which the rule will have to govern, those rules or rights which are not included *expressis verbis* in the treaty continue to exist as customary rules or customary rights. In the former case, the question is one of interpretation of the treaty; but in the latter case, rather than assume that the incidental rule or right, based on custom, is grafted on to the principal rules or rights stated or conferred, or rather re-conferred, by the treaty, it may be a less complicated concept to assume that the wider customary rule continues in existence beside the treaty-rule. It will always be the treaty rule which is invoked or relied on, except in such cases as fall within the area where the treaty and customary law fail to overlap, when it will be the wider pre-existing custom *as a whole* which will be asserted.

When the treaty is only a codifying treaty in the broad sense – when, that is to say, the rules or certain of the rules, which it lays down are not already binding on all States as rules of general customary law – inevitably problems of intertemporal law are likely to arise, as well as problems with regard to relationships with States non-parties to the treaty. A major disadvantage of codifying treaties is that when such multilateral instruments are prepared, as Lord McNair has observed

> "... many States are very willing to authorize their representatives at a conference to sign, but, when the treaty comes home to be studied or pigeonholed by the departments of government concerned, are very dilatory and disappointing in their ratifications".[26]

One cannot therefore, when discussing the effect of codifying treaties on the antecedent law, draw a neat line on the calendar

26. McNair, International Legislation, *XIX Iowa Law Review* (1934) reprinted in *The Law of Treaties,* p. 729ff., at p. 730.

at the point at which the text of a treaty is agreed and signed, nor even at the point when it acquires sufficient ratifications to come into force, and analyse the two situations above and below that line as though they were entirely distinct. Apart from the "staggering" of dates on which the treaty becomes binding as a treaty on each of the States which does eventually ratify it, and the problems of the relationships between the States which have ratified and those which have not yet done so, there may be a considerable period of time between signature of the treaty and the first ratification; this period, and the position of the signatory State which has not yet ratified, are also deserving of some consideration.

The role of an as yet unratified codifying treaty in international law has been well summed up by Professor Baxter:

> "Early in the life of a treaty that is declaratory of customary law but has not yet entered into force, it carries weight as evidence of the state of the law. With the passage of time, its evidentiary force weakens. There still often remains a certain ambiguity about whether the lack of ratifications or accessions comes as the consequence of the fact that States disagree with the treaty or because the treaty has been so warmly received into customary international law that ratification of the treaty or accession to it would be supererogatory",[27]

or, one might add, with the International Court,[28] for some other reason. There can be no doubt that an unratified treaty may be adduced for what it is worth as evidence of the state of general international law; and the answer to the vital question of just what it is worth as such evidence will depend first on to what extent it appears to have been intended to state the law, and to what extent to make changes or reforms, and secondly on the reaction of States to it, insofar as this is susceptible of judicial ascertainment from an examination of, in particular, ratifications or absence of ratifications.

With regard to the question of varying dates of acceptance of the treaty, the complication of the situation results from the fact that the rules laid down in a codifying treaty are general in their content, because the treaty is intended to be of universal application. It is always possible that the activities of States parties to the treaty in question, carried on in accordance with the treaty, may have repercussions on their legal relationships which States which

27. Multilateral Treaties as Evidence of Customary International Law, 41 *B.Y.I.L.* (1965-66), p. 275 at p. 299.

28. "The reasons [for non-ratification] are speculative, but the facts remain": *Continental Shelf* cases, *I.C.J. Reports 1969,* p. 3, at p. 42.

are not, or not yet, parties to the treaty in question.

The point in fact arose in the *Continental Shelf* cases, though in rather an extreme form – a form in which therefore it was not difficult to resolve. The coasts of Denmark and the Netherlands, both countries which had ratified the 1958 Geneva Convention on the Continental Shelf, are situate on each side of the North Sea coast of the Federal Republic of Germany, which had not ratified the Convention. Under Article 6 of the Convention, delimitations of continental shelf areas, between parties to the Convention at least, were, in the absence of agreement to the contrary or special circumstances, to be effected by applying the equidistance principle. Since the Dutch and Danish coasts are practically at right angles to one another, with the German coast in the elbow of the angle, the equidistance technique could be applied, and was applied, by Denmark and the Netherlands to draw a delimitation line which had the effect of leaving very little of the North Sea continental shelf for the Federal Republic.[29] It was then contended by Denmark and the Netherlands that

> "... Denmark and the Netherlands having delimited their continental shelf boundaries specifically on the basis of generally recognised principles and rules of law, these delimitations are prima facie not contrary to international law and are valid with regard to other States".[30]

This argument is a skilful one, because it could apparently be advanced even if the contention also made by the two States concerned, that the "equidistance rule" was in any case binding upon the Federal Republic for the delimitation of the *German* continental shelf, were rejected. The International Court however pointed out that the drawing of the line in question – which in any event could not be justified as based on the Geneva Convention, since this applied only to delimitations between "adjacent States" and "opposite States", and Denmark and the Netherlands in the Court's view were neither – presupposed the delimitation of the German area of the continental shelf by the equidistance method, and this begged the whole question which was at issue in the case.[31]

It must be emphasised that the example is an extreme one; it will serve to draw attention to the difficulties which can arise in

29. See the line EF on the map reproduced at p. 16 of *I.C.J. Reports 1969*.
30. *Continental Shelf* cases, *Pleadings etc.*, Vol. I, p. 177; see also p. 331.
31. *I.C.J. Reports 1969*, p. 28, para. 36.

determining the legal relationships between States which are parties to a codifying treaty and those which are not. As for problems of intertemporal law, another recent case before the International Court of Justice illustrates, again in a somewhat extreme form, the long periods which may elapse – during which the law may develop out of all recognition – between the date when the facts giving rise to an international dispute occur, and the date when the matter falls to be decided by a tribunal. In the *Barcelona Traction* case, ten years passed between the acts complained of, and the first application to the Court, and twenty-one years between the acts complained of and the final judgment in the matter.[32]

It would seem simple enough in theory in such cases to adopt the general rule – itself one of customary international law – that the law to be applied is that in operation at the time of the acts complained of. But the law applicable to the Respondent State may have been general international law, and that applicable to the Applicant State treaty-law under a codifying treaty (or, of course, vice-versa); although the treaty regime could not be applied retrospectively to the Respondent State, it will not be easy at some distance of time, if the treaty-rule has in the meantime passed into general international law, to determine just how much effect the treaty had already had on general law at the time of the acts complained of.

Such intertemporal law problems are difficult to treat *in abstracto,* since much may depend on the content of the treaty, the particular facts, and the attitude of the Respondent State to the treaty at the time. Of more general interest, perhaps, is the position of a State which takes part in the working out of a codifying treaty, but does not ratify, it, vis-à-vis the States which do ratify it.

This point also arose in the *Continental Shelf* cases, the treaty in question again being the 1958 Geneva Convention on the Continental Shelf, and the State being the Federal Republic of Germany, which had nor merely participated in the work of the

32. *I.C.J. Reports 1970,* p. 3. In view of recent misunderstandings on the question of the time element in I.C.J. proceedings, it should perhaps be stressed, first that the claim was not presented for many years because Spain had not yet become a party to the Court's Statute, and secondly that the delays subsequent to the bringing of the claim were due first to a discontinuance and subsequently to requests by the parties for very long periods of time to prepare their pleadings. See *I.C.J. Reports 1970*, pp. 30-31.

Geneva Conference, and signed the Convention – though at the eleventh hour – but had also issued an internal Proclamation announcing its intention to present an Accession Bill to Parliament to enable it to ratify the Convention. It was claimed by Denmark and the Netherlands that these actions by the Federal Republic were, at the least, to be regarded as elements of State practice to be taken into account in deciding whether the "equidistance rule" contained in Article 6 of the Convention was a rule of general international customary law, if not as evidence of specific acceptance of that rule by the Federal Republic as binding upon it.

It is perhaps slightly surprising that the International Court in its Judgment chose to deal with this latter argument, that of acceptance, in isolation, and quite early on in its reasoning, instead of linking it with the more basic question, discussed later in the Judgment, of whether the rule expressed in Article 6 of the Convention was capable of being, and had at any time become, a rule of general international law. The effect of the Court's so treating the "acceptance" argument is to lend colour to the theory that, in other circumstances, as suggested by Professor Baxter,

> "it might . . . be contended that a treaty not yet in force may be employed as evidence of the State practice of the individual State that participated in the drawing up of the agreement and was willing to sign it".[33]

Although the Court rejected the contentions of Denmark and the Netherlands on this point, it did so in language carefully employed so as not exclude the possibility of "a very definite, very consistent course of conduct" on the part of a State in the position of the Federal Republic having the effect claimed.

> "In principle, when a number of States, including the one whose conduct is invoked, and those invoking it, have drawn up a convention specifically providing for a particular method by which the intention to become bound by the régime of the convention is to be manifested – namely by the carrying out of certain prescribed formalities (ratification, accession), it is not lightly to be presumed that a State which has not carried out these formalities, though at all times fully able and entitled to do so, has nevertheless somehow become bound in another way".[34]

Something which "is not lightly to be presumed" is clearly something which can occur; but the Court's view in the particular case was that only the existence of a situation of estoppel could suffice

33. Multilateral Treaties as Evidence of Customary International Law, 41 *B.Y.I.L. (1965-66)*, p. 275 at p. 292.

34. *I.C.J. Reports 1969*, p. 25, para. 28.

to support the view advanced by Denmark and the Netherlands. Estoppel in the true sense of the word[35] there was none; but again, the Court took care not to exclude the possibility that in appropriate cases a State might be estopped by "clearly and consistently evinced acceptance" from disputing the applicability to itself of a treaty regime despite its not having ratified the treaty. Bearing in mind that estoppel in international law is a matter of customary law,[36] we may say that we have here another case in which customary law will be called upon to operate alongside a codified system of law, in order to determine its precise scope and application.

The whole field of the law of treaties, which has up to the present been purely a field governed by customary law, will continue to remain largely an area where customary law is supreme, notwithstanding the preparation of the 1969 Vienna Convention on the Law of Treaties. Apart from the (possibly very lengthy) period of time before that Convention acquires universal or quasi-universal acceptance by States, it must not be overlooked that by Article 4 of the Convention it is provided that

> "Without prejudice to the application of any rules set forth in the present Convention to which treaties would be subject under international law independently of the Convention, the Convention applies only to treaties which are concluded by States after the entry into force of the present Convention with regard to such States".

Even taking into account the vast increase in treaty-making in modern times, and the wide range of subjects to be covered and of transactions to be effected by treaties – which led Lord McNair to refer to the treaty as "the only and sadly overworked instrument with which international society is equipped for the purpose of carrying out its multifarious transactions"[37] – it is clear that it will be a long time before anything like the majority of existing treaties in effective operation will be treaties concluded between States both or all of which are parties to the Vienna Convention of 1969.

35. See D.W. Bowett, Estoppel before International Tribunals and its relation to Acquiescence, 33 *B.Y.I.L.* (1957), p. 176; McNair, *Law of Treaties,* pp. 485-9; Separate Opinion of Sir Gerald Fitzmaurice, *Temple of Preah Vihear, I.C.J. Reports 1962*, p. 52 at pp. 62-65; [MacGibbon, Estoppel in International Law, 7. *I.C.L.Q.* (1958), p. 486.]

36. See Bowett in 33 *B.Y.I.L.* (1957), p. 176 on the development of the concept.

37. The functions and differing legal character of treaties, 11 *B.Y.I.L* (1930), reprinted in *The Law of Treaties,* p. 739ff.

Chapter Eight

CODIFIED LAW AND DISSENTIENT STATES

There is a certain *a priori* unlikeliness about any expectation that a codifying convention in whatever field of law will meet with anything like immediate and universal acceptance, in the form of ratifications and accessions, even if little disagreement has made itself known in the course of the preparation of the text, and even if the treaty is in fact destined to pass, by way of general acceptance, into general international law. One has only to recall the example of the Genocide Convention, which could be regarded as codifying existing customary law,[1] and as to the principles whereof no dissent was voiced: it was adopted by the unanimous vote of fifty-six States. Yet it took ten years for it to obtain fifty-nine ratifications,[2] and during that period the number of existing States making up the international community had increased very considerably; furthermore, by no means all the ratifications deposited were free from reservations, even if only on points of detail.

It is therefore clear that customary law will have a considerable part to play, not merely in the relations *inter se* of States which have not accepted a given codifying treaty, but also in their relations with those which have accepted it; and at the same time the attitude of the dissentient States and the law applied between them will be bound to have an influence on the development of the law laid down by the treaty, and vice versa.

Prior to the conclusion of a codifying treaty, the fact that a certain State, or a certain number of States, disagree with a rule

1. "... the principles underlying the Convention are principles which are recognized by civilized nations as binding on States, even without any conventional obligation". *Reservations to Genocide Convention, I.C.J. Reports 1951*, at p. 23.

2. Cf. Dissenting Opinion of Judge Lachs, *North Sea Continental Shelf, I.C.J. Reports 1969*, at p. 226.

alleged to be a rule of international customary law may be interpreted, according to circumstances, as leading to one of three distinct situations. In the first place, the dissentient State may have maintained its dissent sufficiently consistently and openly from a time when the customary rule alleged had not yet crystallised, for the State concerned to be entitled to claim that the alleged rule, if it exists as part of the general law, cannot be applied to the dissenting State. This was of course one aspect of the Norwegian position in the *Fisheries* case, and in the course of the proceedings it was conceded by the United Kingdom that this contention was sound in law, although it was disputed on the facts.[3] An important qualification to the possible right to resist the application of a customary rule was however indicated by the United Kindom, namely that while a State may acquire an exceptional position with regard to some general *rule* of customary law, there is no such right for a State to isolate itself from the impact of a fundamental *principle.*[4] This contention, which it is suggested is sound, though it was not considered by the Court in the *Fisheries* case, and is not supported by any other case-law, is essentially an assertion of the impossibility of evading, [whether by treaty or by claim to some historic title, the operation of any principle which is either a matter of *jus cogens* or so bound up with the essential nature of a concept of internatioanl law as to be impossible to exclude without denying the existence of the concept.[5]]

Secondly, dissent may have been expressed so effectively by such a number of States that the alleged rule in question will not have acquired the status of a customary law rule at all, or at most will have become a rule of regional or local customary law.[6]

Finally, the dissent of certain States may be wholly ineffective: if there is general acceptance of a practice "as law", and the dissentient States have not made their views heard until after the rule has crystallised and become firmly established, the rule will be binding on all, including the dissentient States.

3. See *Fisheries* case, *Pleadings, Oral Arguments, Documents*,Vol. I, pp. 382-383, and Fitzmaurice in 92 *Recueil des Cours* 1957-II, pp. 99-100.

4. *Fisheries* case, *Pleadings &c.*, Vol. II, pp. 428-429.

5. [See above, pp. 28ff, and below, p. 123. In the *Fisheries* case the Court, by upholding the Norwegian claim, in effect recognised that its method of drawing baselines could not be said to be a denial of the concept of the territorial sea.]

6. On the question of local customary law, see below, pp. 136ff.

Upon one of these pre-existing situations a codifying treaty may be erected, incorporating the rule or rules which are objected to by certain States. In view of their dissent, they will presumably decline to ratify the treaty; they may or may not have participated in its preparation, and if they did so, they may or may not have made their position known. As an alternative to declining to ratify the treaty, they may also ratify it with reservations to the rules which they find unacceptable, assuming that such reservations are permitted by the treaty.

[Before dealing with the question of the effect of the reactions of dissentient States to the completed codifying convention, it may be as well to draw attention to the distorting effects on the text of the convention itself which their supposed participation in the work of the codification conference may have. It might be assumed that there would be an accurate parallelism between the rules which States assert as proper for inclusion in the codifying convention and their own practices in the field to which the convention is to relate; but this would be an over-simplification. Apart from the differing impact of political factors on acts of State practice and on the representations of States at a codifying conference, even legal considerations applied in perfect good faith may have an unexpected effect.

The point is well illustrated by the fate, in the course of the lengthy preparation of what was to be the Vienna Convention on the Law of Treaties, of the question of the so-called "residual rule" as to the need for ratification of a treaty to bring it into force, assuming that the treaty itself does not state whether or not ratification is required. There has for many years been controversy as to whether in such a case the presumption, or "residual rule", is that the States parties are bound merely by their signatures, or that they must be taken to have intended ratification to be necessary to bring the treaty into effect. In particular it has been argued by Sir Gerald Fitzmaurice[7] that the view that in such cases ratification must be taken to be necessary was unsupported by practice, and that the true rule was that

> "Treaties are subject to ratification in all those cases where they so specify; otherwise, in general, they are not. There is no principle or rule of law according

7. Do Treaties need Ratification?, 15*B.Y.I.L.* (1934), p. 113; First Report on the Law of Treaties, *ILC Yearbook* 1956-II, pp. 104ff., at pp. 123-124.

> to which treaties are tacitly to be assumed to be subject to ratification, whether this is provided for or not".[8]

Whether this is a true expression of international law on the point is not here to the purpose;[9] at all events, Sir Gerald Fitzmaurice's view carries authority, and for the purposes of argument it will be assumed that, in particular, he was correct in asserting that

> "States . . . have always insisted on providing expressly for ratification in those cases where they wanted it; while on the other hand being quite content to rely on silence precisely in those cases where they did not want it"[10]

In the course of the discussions in the International Law Commission on the law of treaties, this view of the "residual rule" was strongly opposed, and it was so opposed by, *inter alios*, those who had the interests and the practice of the South American States in mind. The problem for these States was that their constitutions provided for parliamentary approval to be obtained for treaties on important matters as a preliminary to ratification,[11] and there appeared to be a danger, if it were accepted in the proposed codifying convention that the residual rule was that signature was sufficient to bind the States parties to a treaty, that the parliamentary processes required by the constitution of such a State might be by-passed.[12]

The whole history of the controversy need not be gone into here: an excellent account has been given by Professor Briggs in his recent Hague Lectures;[13] but the final outcome, due, at least in part, to the attitude of the Latin American States, was the inclusion of what are now Articles 12 and 14 of the Vienna Convention of the Law of Treaties, which deal with the matter in such a way as to make no provision for a residual rule, i.e., the conflict is left unresolved. If it is assumed, for the purposes of argument, that there is a residual rule, and that it is as postulated by Sir Gerald Fitzmaurice, the attitude of the Latin American

8. Article 32, para. 2, of draft Code, *ILC Yearbook* 1956-II, p. 113.

9. Cf. Blix, The Requirement of Ratification, 30 *B.Y.I.L.* (1953), p. 352, at p. 365: "The only – somewhat unhelpful – conclusion which can be drawn from the practice . . . is probably that the residuary rule is not very well established."

10. *ILC Yearbook*, 1956-II, at p. 123.

11. See U.N. Legislative Series, Laws and Practices concerning the Conclusion of Treaties, ST/LEG/SER.B/3.

12. See *ILC Yearbook* 1950-I, at p. 65 (Mr. Amado); 1962-I, at p. 100 (Mr. Jiménez de Aréchaga) and p. 101 (Mr. Paredes).

13. Reflections on the Codification of International Law by the International Law Commission and by Other Agencies, 126 *Recueil des Cours*, 1969-I, pp. 244ff.

States, and the effect on the Vienna Convention – which is at least in part understood to be codifying *stricto sensu*[14] – of that attitude, is extremely illuminating for our discussion. The constitutional problems of those States were, in the field of actual State practice capable of giving rise to or supporting a rule of customary law, wholly ineffective to influence the customary rule, since, as Sir Gerald Fitzmaurice had pointed out,[15] they would always take the precaution of providing for ratification if they considered that ratification would be required; or if such problems did influence the creation and stability of the rule, they would tend to reinforce a rule that signature was sufficient unless otherwise specified.

Thus legal considerations affecting a particular group of States the effect of which in the actual practice of States would, if anything, be to strengthen an alleged rule of customary law, operated through the machinery of codification to weaken it to a considerable extent, if not to suppress it, by its exclusion from the codifying convention. It is thus apparent that there may be an important qualitative difference between the conduct of States in their everyday relations, and their attitude in the course of codification of a branch of law, so far as the effect thereof on existing and developing customary law is concerned.]

Nonetheless it is clear that in pure legal theory, the conclusion of a codifying treaty – if we take it to set out unchanged the rules which are accepted by the majority of States but objected to by some, and which is therefore a codifying treaty in the strict sense – neither adds anything to nor subtracts anything from the legal situation existing prior to the conclusion of the treaty, so far as the position of the dissentient States is concerned. If the rule in question was already a rule of general international law, binding on those States, it is not abrogated for being codified;[16] if it was not such a rule, then it is unlikely to have "crystallised" as such merely by virtue of the working-out of the treaty, if no more States demonstrate their acceptance of it than had accepted it prior to the treaty.

14. [See preamble to the Vienna Convention: "Believing that the codification and progressive development of the law of treaties achieved in the present convention . . ." See also *Legal Consequences for States of the Continued Presence of South Africa in Namibia (South West Africa) I.C.J. Reports 1971,* at p. 47, para. 94.]

15. [See above, note 10.)]

16. [See above, p. 100; whatever the situation between parties to a treaty, it cannot abrogate a general rule as regards non-parties.]

Nevertheless, there can be no doubt that to a certain extent, paucity of ratifications, and the attachment of reservations to ratifications do in the case of a *soi-disant* codifying treaty have a decidedly weakening effect on the rules set out in the treaty. The matter is essentially one of evidence: unless the existence of the rule in question as a rule of customary law has already been clearly established, in particular by the decision of an international tribunal,[17] before the conclusion of the treaty, a tribunal considering the question at any subsequent time will be bound to consider all circumstances which may be relevant as evidence for or against the claim that the rule is one of general international law. It is not a question of establishing the existence of the rule at some particular point in time, in the past, and then considering whether subsequent events may show it to have become weakened or abrogated; on this basis, it is clear that the maintenance of an objection by refusal to ratify the convention which enshrines the rule could not, as already mentioned, modify the pre-existing situation. A tribunal must on the contrary consider whether the rule claimed existed at the time of the dispute, and must weigh all the evidence for and against, including ratifications given and refused to the codifying convention, only excluding acts of the parties after the "critical date"[18] with regard to the dispute before the tribunal.

Thus in the *Asylum* case, the International Court of Justice observed:

> "It is contended that this Convention [the 1933 Montevideo Convention] has merely codified principles which were already recognized by Latin-American custom, and that it is valid . . . as a proof of customary law. The limited number of States which have ratified this Convention reveals the weakness of this argument . . ."[19]

Similarly, in the *North Sea Continental Shelf* case, discussing the contention that the 1958 Geneva Convention on the Continental

17. "The imprimatur given to a customary rule of international law by the International Court of Justice would suffice to clinch its recognition in most cases" Briggs, The Columbian-Peruvian Asylum case and Proof of Customary International Law, 45 *A.J.I.L.* (1951), p. 728 at p. 729.

18. On the "critical" date, cf. *Minquiers and Ecrehou, I.C.J. Reports 1953*, p. 59. Cf. also the allegations against the Federal Republic of Germany of having changed its tune when the possibility of dispute became apparent, in *North Sea Continental Shelf, Pleadings &c.*, Vol. I, p. 212, para. 153 and p. 365, para. 148.

19. *I.C.J. Reports 1950,* p. 277.

Shelf had crystallised customary law on the subject, or had by virtue of subsequent practice passed into general law, the Court observed that the number of ratifications received by the Convention was insuffucient to justify such a conclusion, and continued:

> "That non-ratification may sometimes be due to factors other than active disapproval of the convention concerned can hardly constitute a basis on which positive acceptance of its principles can be implied: the reasons are speculative, but the facts remain".[20]

Thus just as the mere convening of a codification conference may easily have the effect of throwing up disagreements on what had until then always been considered reasonably well settled rules of existing customary law; so also the conclusion of a codifying treaty may, unless the rules it embodies have already been so clearly settled as to be more or less unchallengeable – in which case there will be little point in concluding the treaty – have the immediate effect of shaking the authority of those rules.[21]

The underlying reason is that if the ratification of a codifying treaty can constitute both an act of State practice and evidence of the *opinio juris* for the assessment of the status of an alleged rule of international customary law,[22] then it is impossible not to regard abstention from ratification, if it is suffiently widespread, and not otherwise clearly explicable, also as State practice and as evidence of "negative *opinio juris*", i.e. the absence of belief in the rule as a rule of customary law, or the belief in some other rule.[23] Naturally, more caution is necessary – as the International Court emphasises in the passage quoted above – in assessing the probative value of abstention than in assessing ratifications, which are positive acts. But the conclusion of a codifying treaty affords all States to which the treaty is opened for signature the opportunity

20. *I.C.J. Reports 1969*, p. 42, para. 73. See also the examination of the question in the dissenting opinion of Judge Lachs, ibid., pp. 226ff.

21. [Cf. Ago, La codification du droit international, *En hommage à Paul Guggenheim,* 1968, p. 93 at p. 110, quoting the case of the Conventions drawn up at the 1958 Geneva Conference on the Law of the Sea.]

22. See above, p. 85ff.

23. [Contra, Zemanek, Die Bedeutung der Kodifizierung des Völkerrechts für seine Anwendung, *Festschrift Verdross*, p. 565 at pp. 589-590, whose conclusion is that "infolge der Unsicherheit in der Beurteilung der Motive, die Staaten von der Beteiligung an kodifikatorischen Konventionen abhalten, aus der Nichtbeteiligung kein Urteil über den Bestand des in den Konventionen kodifizierten Gewohnheitsrechts gefällt werden kann".]

of making their contribution, positively or negatively, to the corpus of State practice on the subject, by ratifying, ratifying with reservations or declining to ratify, as the case may be. There is thus a sudden acceleration of the process by which a customary rule comes into existence and grows, an acceleration which will usually be favourable to the crystallisation of the custom as law, but which may, if enough States are opposed or indifferent, prove to be unfavourable.

The position of dissentient States which are in a small minority may, on the other hand, be made more difficult by the conclusion of a codifying treaty setting out rules with which they disagree. In the normal course of inter-State relations, the State which declines to accept an emerging rule of general law has to object to its application to itself, consistently and openly, from the time when the rule begins to settle down.[24] It is however only bound to make its position known insofar as the application of the emerging rule to the objecting State's own interests is concerned; thus in the instance afforded by the *Fisheries* case, Norway could only be required to have insisted on the non-application of the alleged general rule to its own coasts, and was not expected to have made protests when other States applied the alleged general rule to their own coasts. But when a codifying treaty effects the sudden acceleration of usage to which we have just referred, the "acts" of State practice involved are not in any way acts which purport to "apply" the rule to States non-parties to the treaty, and leave no room for a dissentient State to do more than attach a reservation to its own ratification, or decline to ratify altogether. Thus the dissentient State will be deprived of the opportunity of maintaining open and consistent protest, and may find it difficult to resist the application of the general rule to its own interests at a subsequent date.

It would appear that a dissentient State which participates in the work of a codification conference can at least be expected to make its views known: this was the view of Lord McNair, who, in his dissenting opinion in the *Fisheries* case, pointed out that the Norwegian delegate to the 1881 North Sea Conference might have been expected, if the peculiar method of drawing base-lines claimed by Norway had then been practised, to have disclosed its

24. See above, p. 110.

existence to the Conference.[25]

A more complex problem which it will be for general customary law to resolve is that of the effect of reservations to ratifications of multilateral codifying treaties, and the possibility of making such reservations at all in many cases. An orderly set of rules on this subject are to be found in Articles 19 to 23 of the 1969 Vienna Convention on the Law of Treaties, but it is difficult, in the light of the views of the various Special Rapporteurs for the International Law Commission on the subject,[26] to regard these rules as themselves a codification – in the strict sense – of the existing law on the subject.

It will be recalled that up to the time when the International Court gave its Advisory opinion on the question of *Reservations to the Genocide Convention*,[27] there was considerable consensus of opinion that the same rule applied with regard to reservations to multilateral conventions as applied to ordinary bilateral treaties, namely that no reservation could be regarded as valid, so that the State making the reservation would become a party to the treaty, subject to the reservation, unless and until the reservation had been accepted by all the other States parties to the treaty. The opinion given by the International Court however – subject to the powerful dissent of Judges Guerrero, McNair, Read and Hsu Mo, and Judge Alvarez, – was that that rule, if it was a general rule, did not apply in the particular case of the Genocide Convention. In the light of the intentions of those who framed the treaty, the Court advised that

> "a State which has made and maintained a reservation which has been objected to by one or more of the parties to the Convention but not by others, can be regarded as being a party to the Convention if the reservation is compatible with the object and purpose of the Convention; otherwise, that State cannot be regarded as being a party to the Convention;"[28]

and that

> "if a party to the Convention objects to a reservation which it considers to be incompatible with the object and purpose of the Convention, it can in fact consider that the reserving State is not a party to the Convention"[28]

25. *I.C.J. Reports 1951*, p. 158 at pp. 178-179.
26. See in particular the Report of the last Rapporteur (Sir Humphrey Waldock) in *I.L.C. Yearbook 1962*, Vol. II, p. 27, particularly pp. 62-68 and 73-80.
27. *I.C.J. Reports 1951*, p. 15.
28. *Ibid.*, at p. 29.

The Opinion of the Court is of course of extremely weighty authority, but it was, as the Court itself emphasised,[29] confined to the particular Convention upon which its opinion had been asked. Particularly in the light of the joint Dissenting Opinion of Judges Guerrero, McNair, Read and Hsu Mo, which was based on the view that the rule requiring universal acceptance of a reservation by the parties to the treaty was in fact an existing rule of general law,[30] to which the Genocide Convention was no exception,[31] it would seem to be correct to say that except where a contrary intention on the part of those who framed the treaty is shown or can be presumed, the rule of universal acceptance is the general rule still, and the criterion of "object and purpose" is applicable only in the case of conventions to which it must be presumed to have been intended by the framers of the treaty to apply.[32] It was in fact common ground between the majority of the Court and the authors of the joint dissenting opinion that whether the rule of universal acceptance or some other rule applied to the Genocide Convention depended on the will of the original parties who drew up the treaty. For this reason, the question whether the object and purpose rule is applicable to general codifying treaties is not one which can be answered in general and abstract terms; there are however certain general observations which may be made.

There is of course a definite distinction to be made between the intention of the States which have drawn up a convention to permit of reservations being made to it, and the intention of the same States to require – or not to require – that such reservations obtain universal acceptance before the reserving State can be regarded as a party to the treaty. If all the States parties do in fact accept a given reservation, the question of whether it was originally intended that reservations be permitted becomes wholly academic, since the universal agreement of the parties to the treaty can always alter what was originally intended; but otherwise the two questions which must be asked successively are: were reserva-

29. "... the replies which the Court is called upon to give ... are necessarily and strictly limited to that Convention": *ibid.*, at p. 20.

30. *I.C.J. Reports 1951*, p. 31 at p. 41.

31. *Ibid.*, at p. 43.

32. Cf. O'Connell, *International Law*, Vol. I, p. 253: [Lauterpacht, Report on the Law of Treaties, *ILC Yearbook 1953*-II, p. 123.]

tions to be permitted at all? if so, were they to be subject to universal acceptance to be effective?

In the *Genocide Convention* case, the International Court appears to have considered that a positive answer to the first of these two questions implied a negative answer to the second; the Court said that

> "it has been argued that there exists a rule of international law subjecting the effect of a reservation to the express or tacit consent of all the contracting parties . . . This view, however, cannot prevail if . . . it can be established that the parties intended to derogate from that rule by admitting the faculty to make reservations . . ." [33]

Read literally, this would seem to mean that if the States responsible for the preparation of a Convention can be shown to have contemplated the faculty of making reservations to the convention, they must also have intended that the universal acceptance rule should not apply. The underlying argument appears to be that if the universal acceptance rule were to apply in such circumstances, the agreement of the authors of the convention that reservations would be permitted would lose most of its meaning, since every reservation would require the express consent of every other party to the convention.

It is suggested that this conclusion is of doubtful validity. If the parties originally intended the universal acceptance rule to apply, then, as already mentioned, their original agreement that reservations would be permissible would certainly not take the matter much farther; but nonetheless, the intitial stage of agreeing to permit reservations does have a real meaning, as a sort of *pactum de contrahendo*, obliging the parties to it not to dismiss any reservations to ratifications of the convention out of hand, but to consider whether (for example) they are consistent with the object and purpose of the treaty.

If, or to the extent that, a codifying treaty is codifying in the narrow sense of setting out existing rules of customary law, it might be expected that reservations to the treaty, or to so much of it as represented existing customary law, would either not be permissible at all, that is to say would be expressly or impliedly excluded by the treaty, or would be foredoomed to rejection as incompatible with the "object and purpose" of the treaty. This

33. *I.C.J. Reports 1951,* at p. 24.

view is supported by the recent dictum of the International Court that

> "... speaking generally, it is a characteristic of purely conventional rules and obligations that, in regard to them, some faculty of making unilateral reservations may, within certain limits, be admitted; – whereas this cannot be so in the case of general or customary law rules and obligations which, by their very nature, must have equal force for all members of the international community, and cannot therefore be the subject of any right of unilateral exclusion exerciseable at will by any one of them in its own favour. Consequently, it is to be expected that when, for whatever reason, rules or obligations of this order are embodied, or are intended to be reflected in certain provisions of a convention, such provisions will figure amongst those in respect of which a right of unilateral reservation is not conferred or is excluded".[34]

But it may be asked whether this statement is not in fact somewhat too wide.

While it is true that "general or customary law rules and obligations" must "by their very nature ... have equal force for all members of the international community", in the sense that if they do not, they cannot be general rules of law at all, but at most rules of local or special customary law, this requirement is satisfied if the rules in question are generally recognized as such by the members of the international community; it does not also imply that they must in all cases be observed, and can in no circumstances be waived or excluded by agreement between two or more States.[35] The whole significance of the distinction between *jus dispositivum* and *jus cogens* is that rules of law falling within the former category may freely be varied or excluded by agreement in the relations between two or more States, provided the position of third-party States is in no way prejudiced.

Furthermore, the reference, in the passage just quoted, to a purported "right of unilateral exclusion exerciseable at will" by a State party to a multilateral convention, while – as we shall

34. *North Sea Continental Shelf* cases, *I.C.J. Reports 1969*, p. 3, at pp. 38-39.

35. [Thus Professor Zemanék considers that the *Continental Shelf* Judgment betrays an underlying confusion with the concept of *jus cogens*: see Die Bedeutung der Kodifizierung des Völkerrechts für seine Anwendung, *Festschrift Verdross*, p. 565, at p. 584, note 84. However, Professor Zemanek appears to have understood the Court to be asserting that if existing rules of customary international law are stated in a codifying Convention, a clause will be inserted barring reservations to the relevant Articles; but all the Court said was that one would expect such Articles to be included in the list of those to which reservations are excluded, if provision is made for barring reservations at all. Thus the absence of a reservations clause in the other 1958 Geneva Conventions does not invalidate the point made in the Judgment.]

see – it is intelligible in the particular case of the 1958 Geneva Convention on the Continental Shelf, is misleading if read as a general statement. A reservation is of course from its inception a unilateral act; but it is a cardinal principle of any theory as to the legal effect of reservations to multilateral treaties that no State can be bound vis-à-vis a reserving State without the consent of the first State;[36] thus a reservation can only take effect if it is accepted by one or more of the other States parties to the relevant treaty, so that from being a unilateral act, it becomes bilateral or multilateral.

Thus a reservation to a multilateral treaty which is accepted by one or more of the other parties to the treaty creates a *lex specialis* operative solely between the reserving State and those States which have accepted the reservation, in exactly the same way as if the States concerned had entered into a wholly separate treaty on the same subject to regulate their mutual relations. Provided the position of the other States parties to the treaty is safeguarded, and provided that the rules varied or excluded are not matters of *jus cogens*, the reservation may be perfectly valid and effective, notwithstanding the fact that it departs from rules which, prior to and outside the multilateral convention, are rules of general customary law.

Thus it is not to be presumed that because a treaty sets out existing rules of customary international law, the parties thereto must have intended to exclude any possibility of making reservations to such of its provisions as re-state general law, nor that they must be taken to have subjected such reservations to the "universal acceptance" rule. The question of the 1958 Geneva Convention on the Continental Shelf was an exceptional one, for reasons which must be mentioned, since that Convention typifies an exception to the principles just mentioned which may be met with in other conventions.

Article 12 of the Geneva Convention provides that

> "any State may make reservations to articles of the Convention other than to Articles 1 to 3 inclusive".[37]

36. See for example, [Bishop, Reservations to Treaties, 103 *Recueil des Cours*, 1961-II, at p. 337;] O'Connell, *International Law*, Vol. I, p. 255; [Oppenheim-Lauterpacht, Vol. I, p. 914; Verdross, *Völkerrecht*, p. 166; Cavaré, *Droit international positif*, Vol. II, p. 123.]

37. See *North Sea Continental Shelf, Pleadings & c.*, Vol. I, pp. 223 at 225.

The argument before the Court was directed to the significance of the fact that reservations were thus permitted to Article 6, which it was claimed re-stated or had crystallised existing customary law. However, as Sir Humphrey Waldock observed in the course of his argument,

> "the reservations clause was introduced in Article 12 more for the purpose of prohibiting reservations to Articles 1,2 and 3 than of authorizing reservations to Articles 4 to 7"[38]

although no-one disputed that it did in fact have the latter effect. Articles 1 to 3 were however different in nature from the rest of the convention,[39] and from the majority of provisions in multilateral codifying treaties of the kind we have been considering; they did not relate in any way to the conduct of States parties to the convention, nor to the rights and obligations *inter se*; they provided a definition of what the continental shelf is, as understood in international law, and what rights are, by virtue of the convention, to be regarded as belonging to the coastal State in respect of the area of continental shelf appertaining to it.

It will thus be apparent why it was inevitable that reservations to Articles 1 to 3 of the Convention should be totally excluded. As we have seen, there is no reason why a reservation which acts as a variation, between particular States, of a rule of conduct, or as a waiver of a right or obligation operating between States, should not be made despite the customary law nature of the rule, right or obligation so varied or waived. But just as it would not be possible – assuming the precepts laid down in Articles 1 to 3 of the Geneva Convention to represent established general law – for a State to disown its area of continental shelf, or for a landlocked State to claim such an area, regardless of the attitude of the neighbouring States, so no reservation could be possible which would amount to a denial of the customary law concept of the continental shelf; and practically any reservation to Articles 1 to 3 would be tantamount to such a denial.[40]

We must conclude that in considering whether or not reservations can be possible to provisions in a codifying treaty which

38. *Ibid.*, Vol. II, p. 107-108.

39. [See also Nordquist, The Legal Status of Articles 1-3 of the Continental Shelf Convention According to the North Sea Cases, *California Western International Law Journal*, Vol. I (1970), p. 60.]

40. [See above, pp. 28ff.]

state existing general international law, it is necessary to distinguish first between matters of *jus dispositivum* and matters of *jus cogens*, and secondly between reservations designed to create a special regime between the reserving States and any other States which are willing to accept it, and reservations which are equivalent to a denial that a concept of genral law exists, or has the content attributed to it by the general law. In this connection, however, it is the substance of the reservation which must be looked to, and not merely the form; experience shows that when States find a rule of law inconvenient, they are apt to denounce it, and deny its force as a rule of law, rather than admit its force, but endeavour to agree a divergent regime; so a reservation which in terms denies that a given rule in a codifying treaty is a rule of general international law, and proceeds to exclude its application to the reserving State, may be read as meaning no more than an invitation to other States to waive that rule in their relations with the reserving State.

There remains the question of the "object and purpose" test; since, as noted above, the application of this test depends on the will of the authors of the convention in question, there is not a lot that can be said about its applicability in general to codifying treaties. It may however be noted that the object and purpose of a codifying treaty may be expressed in two different ways. If the purpose of a codifying treaty, *stricto sensu*, is to re-state the existing law in a clear, systematic and easily accessible form, then such purpose is not interfered with by the attaching of reservations to ratifications of the treaty; such reservations are particular to the reserving State, and as reservations, only operate for the future, so that (subject to what has been said above about the weakening effect of paucity of ratifications, or unfettered ratifications)[41] the force and content of the general law is not affected.

If, on the other hand, the object of the treaty can be said to be to ensure consistency and uniformity in the activities of States in the field of law governed by the treaty, it might be arguable that reservations – any reservations – to the treaty would be contrary to its object and purpose.[42] But it is difficult to see, in the abstract, how a codifying treaty could hope to impose a greater

41. See above, p. 114.

42. [In this sense, see Zemanek, Die Bedeutung der Kodifizierung des Völkerrechts für seine Anwendung, *Festschrift Verdross*, p. 565 at p. 585.]

degree of uniformity and consistency than had already been found appropriate by States in the course of the development of the customary rules which the treaty was designed to codify; and the exclusion of reservations would be likely to lead to few ratifications being deposited, the remaining States being more content to be bound by the former customary law, or by specific agreements between themselves operating entirely outside the treaty.

Chapter Nine

CODIFICATION AND AFTER: THE SUBSEQUENT DEVELOPMENT OF THE LAW

A vital problem which can hardly fail to arise between parties to a multilateral codifying treaty, in a more acute form than as between parties to any other form of treaty, whether bilateral or multilateral, is that of the development of the law governing the relationships between the parties, in the field covered by the treaty, subsequent to the coming into force of the treaty. It would clearly be rash to assume that international law in codified form, however great the care and effort with which the codifying instrument is prepared and drafted, will remain the most satisfactory solution of the problems with which it attempts to grapple, whatever changes may occur in international relationships. One of the principal arguments used in favour of codification of law as against the processes of the customary law is the slowness with which custom normally develops: but slow development is at all events preferable to fixity, since *tempora mutantur et nos mutamur in illis.* Nor can it be supposed that the general law after the conclusion of a codifying treaty will continue to develop as though nothing had happened; it was conceded by one of the most arrent supporters of the codification of international law that codification

> "certainly interferes with the so-called organic growth of the law through usage into custom".[1]

The difficulty is of course that customary law develops of its own accord, without there being any need for States to do more than continue their day-to-day relations, whereas a treaty regime can only be changed by deliberate act of the parties. Furthermore, as Professor Baxter has observed,

1. Oppenheim, *International Law* (8th Edition by Lauterpacht), Vol. I, pp. 58-59.

"The clear formulation of rules in a codification treaty and the assent of a substantial number of States may have the effect of arresting change and flux in the state of customary international law. Although the treaty 'photographs' the state of the law at the time of its entry into force as to individual States, it continues, so long as States remain parties to it, to speak in terms of the present".[2]

Thus so far as the States non-parties to the treaty are concerned, for whom the codifying treaty is only evidence of the state of customary law at a certain moment in time, a "photograph" in Professor Baxter's vivid expression, other evidence, in particular of practice since the treaty, may show that for such States the law has not stood still: but the treaty will remain strong evidence, not easy to controvert, that the law is still as the treaty states it, so that the treaty will undoubtedly have a freezing effect on the customary law even for States non-parties to it.

For the States parties to the treaty, change can only come about by amendment, revision or modification of the treaty.[3] Whether or not a multilateral treaty provides for its own revision – and such provision is nowadays fairly common practice – it is certain that the agreement of all parties to the treaty can modify it to whatever extent is desired, so as in effect to substitute a new treaty for the old one. The disadvantages of revision by universal agreement, which may entail calling a fresh codification conference, are well known: as Sir Humphrey Waldock has observed,

"international treaty-making practice show[s] a definite tendency to maintain old treaties in being as far as possible so as not to lose the benefit of the ratifications slowly accumulated over the years".[4]

Until a complete set of ratifications of the amending treaty are obtained from the parties to the old treaty, the new treaty cannot take the place of, or supplement, the old; it was this difficulty that impelled the Council of the League of Nations, on 23 January 1936, to take the unusual step of deciding that the Protocol amending the Statute of the Permanent Court of International

2. Multilateral Treaties as Evidence of Customary International Law, 41 *B.Y.I.L.* (1965-66), p. 275 at p. 299.

3. For this reason, there is something to be said for the codification of law by declaration – provided it is made perfectly clear that the declaration does not purport to be more than a statement by the States parties to it that the contents of the declaration are what they understand the current law on the subject to be – since they are not then committed to that law *in aeternum*. However, declarations doing no more than state agreed and definite existing law are not really a practical proposition: see above, p. 18.

4. *Yearbook of the I.L.C.*, 1964 Vol. I, p. 154, para. 23.

Justice should come into effect for all parties to the Statute (since the changes it made were such that it could not take effect only for those States which agreed, and not for others) unless by a certain date objection had been made by any of the three States parties to the Statute which had failed to deposit ratifications of the Protocol, thus delaying its coming into force on the date originally planned, and causing various problems of intertemporal law.[5]

However, the traditional rule for modification of multilateral treaties is and remains that the consent of the parties – all the parties – to the original treaty is required; but as Sir Humphrey Waldock, the last of several Special Rapporteurs on the Law of Treaties, observed in his Report to the International Law Commission,

> "History furnishes many instances of treaty regimes amended or revised by a new treaty concluded between some only of the parties to the earlier treaty . . . The rule requiring the unanimous consent of all the original parties for revision . . . has in the past been honoured more in the breach than in the observance".[6]

Thus the 1969 Vienna Convention on the Law of Treaties draws a careful distinction between the *amendment* of multilateral treaties (Article 40 of the Convention), for which unanimity continues to be required,[7] and the *modification* of such treaties by agreement between certain of the parties only. The latter process is regarded as proper, and permitted by the Vienna Convention, if it is authorized by the original treaty, or if it is not prohibited by the original treaty and the following two conditions are satisfied, namely that the modification

> "(i) does not affect the enjoyment by the other parties of their rights under the treaty or the performance of their obligations;
> (ii) does not relate to a provision, derogation from which is incompatible with the effective execution of the object and purpose of the treaty as a whole".[8]

The first of these two sub-paragraphs simply re-states, with particular reference to treaties modifying (to adopt the convenient terminology of the Convention) earlier treaties, the basic principle

5. See Manley Hudson, *The Permanent Court of International Justice, 1920-1942,* pp. 136-141.

6. Third Report on the Law of Treaties, *I.L.C. Yearbook,* 1964, Vol. II, at p. 49.

7. On the unanimity rule, see E.C. Hoyt, *The Unanimity Rule in the Revision of Treaties: a Re-examination* (1959), and J. Leca, *Les techniques de révision des conventions internationales* (1961), at pp. 158ff.

8. Vienna Convention, Article 41, para. 1.

of general law that *pacta tertiis nec nocent nec prosunt.* The criterion laid down in the second sub-paragraph, that of the "object and purpose of the treaty as a whole", will be recognised as borrowed from the law of reservations to multilateral treaties, and in particular from the Advisory Opinion of the International Court of Justice in the case concerning *Reservations to the Genocide Convention.*[9] We have already discussed this criterion with regard to the problem of reservations to codifying treaties,[10] and would merely recall here the possible distinction to be made between treaties of which the object is simply to state the law, and treaties whose object is to render its observation uniform.

It would seem reasonable to suppose that in the future, and particularly with regard to codifying treaties which, if they truly reflect legal rules which are, or come to be, widely accepted, may be expected to receive ratification by a large number of States, it will in fact be less common for subsequent treaties to be concluded to amend the principal treaty than for them to be devised to modify it.[11] When proposals are made for the general amendment of such a treaty (and since the treaty is, by its nature, assumed to be of identical interest to all States,[12] this is really the more logical course), it will be realistic to assume that for what may be a very considerable period such an agreement will only operate in the way contemplated by paragraphs 4 and 5 of Article 40 of the Vienna Convention: that is to say, the amending agreement will be binding between such States as have ratified it, and the original treaty will remain binding between States which have not ratified the amending instrument, as well as between States which have ratified that instrument, on the one hand, and States which have not, on the other.

The paradoxical result to which these observations lead is that in the long run the objective of ensuring unity of practice and obligation in international law will be more effectively achieved if the matters in question are left to the slow accumulation and

9. *I.C.J. Reports 1951*, p. 15.

10. See above, p. 117, 123.

11. An example is the 1967 Protocol relating to the Status of Refugees: see Weis in *B.Y.I.L.* 1967, p. 40ff., in particular at p. 59: "The procedure for revision of the 1951 Convention . . . was not resorted to in view of the urgency . . . and of the fact that the amended treaty would have required fresh consent by the States parties to the Convention."

12. Note that Article 41, paragraph 2, requires States who agree to modify an earlier treaty *inter se* to notify the other parties.

growth of custom, than if the device of a codifying treaty is adopted. Such a treaty will give a more immediate consistency to practices which, if sufficiently in harmony to justify codification, yet show such a degree of diversity as to make codification advantageous; but such immediate consistency will last only as long as the codifying treaty continues to meet all the requirements of the international community in that field, and will subsequently in all probability give way to two or even more inconsistent regimes; and unity is unlikely to be achieved again for a very considerable time. In contrast, changes in customary international law, although it is not possible to plot their course as precisely as that of changes in rules of conventional origin and basis, do adapt the "original" customary rule with regard to all members of the international community, so that the essential unity of international law on the subject in question is preserved.

The conflicts which may arise from the development of international law by the revision of codifying treaties, or their modification by some only of the parties, are, as Dr. Jenks has observed,[13] only examples of a wider category of conflicts between "law-making" treaties, most of which however fall rather outside the scope of the present study. As Dr. Jenks points out

> "The possibility of conflict is not limited to instruments of different types, instruments of different geographical scope, instruments approaching a problem from different angles, and instruments dealing with different subjects or aspects of a subject which are related to each other; one of the most important types of conflict to be considered consists of conflicts between an original and a revised instrument, or between successive revisions of an instrument which is of the same potential scope but is in fact in force for different groups of parties".[14]

Clearly the only tool available to aid the resolution of such conflicts between treaty-instruments is in fact international customary law with regard to the interpretation and application of treaties generally, possibly supplemented in the future between such States as are parties to it, by the relevant provisions of the Vienna Convention on the Law of Treaties.[15]

As Dr. Jenks concludes on this point:

> "In any case, it would seem clear that, given the complex structure and interrelations of contemporary law-making treaties, no State can reasonably claim to

---

13. The Conflict of Law-Making Treaties, 30 *B.Y.I.L.* (1953) p. 401.
14. *Op. cit.*, at p. 418.
15. See Articles 30,31 and 59.

> abrogate unilaterally an obligation under any such treaty on the ground of an alleged inconsistency therewith of, or an alleged violation of the terms thereof by, another treaty. Any such question, if not settled by agreement between the parties or organizations concerned, must be regarded as one for judicial determination",[16]

and a tribunal which is called upon to decide such a question can only apply general rules of interpretation, coupled with the general principle that treaties are only effective between the parties. Dr. Jenks has suggested in his paper a number of principles which might be found useful in endeavouring to settle problems of conflict between law-making treaties,[17] but he concedes that

> "none of these principles has any absolute validity, or can be applied automatically and mechanically to any particular class of case".[18]

This is clearly a field of law in which development can only result from experience of the methods applied and found effective in various classes of case.

A question which is more delicate is that of the impact of continuing development of customary law on codified rules, inasmuch as custom is likely to diverge steadily from the rules laid down in black and white in the codifying treaty or instrument. This is in effect the question of the operation of custom *contra legem* referred to above:[19] to what extent is modification of a codifying treaty by custom possible, either as between particular parties or generally?

Where codification has been effected by multilateral treaty, the question is essentially how a practice contrary to or which diverges from the treaty can become established, with the necessary concomitant *opinio juris*, so as to create a customary rule, and how the subsequent customary rule can over-ride the quasi-legislative provisions of the treaty. This is not by any means a novel difficulty: in terms of general legal philosophy it was, for example discussed by St. Thomas Aquinas[20] in the Summa Theologica; and

16. 30 *B.Y.I.L.* (1953) p. 401 at p. 435.

17. The hierarchic principle, the *lex prior* principle, the *lex posterior* principle, the *lex specialis* principle, the autonomous operation principle, the "pith and substance" principle, and the legislative intention principle. See *op. cit.*, pp. 436-450.

18. *Op. cit.*, p. 453.

19. See above, p. 98.

20. Summa, II-I, Quaestio XCVII, Art. III, 2. Quotations from Roman edition of 1894: "Ex multis malis non potest fieri unum bonum: sed ille, qui incipit primo contra

Aquinas' answer to the problem is of sufficient interest to be worth quoting.

The difficulty, expressed in Aquinas' terms, is that two or more wrongs do not make a right: how can an accumulation of acts contrary to existing law abrogate that law and give rise to a new rule of customary law? Aquinas' answer is as follows:

> "Human laws prove inadequate in particular cases; it is therefore sometimes possible to act alongside the law (*praeter legem*), that is to say, in those cases in which the law is found wanting, and yet so to act will not be wrongful. When such cases become frequent as a result of some change in human affairs, it becomes manifest through custom that the law is no longer appropriate (*utilis*), just as it would become manifest that this was the case if a specific new law to the contrary were promulgated".[21]

Thus when custom *praeter legem* begins, as a result of social development, so to encroach on the existing law's domain as to verge on the *contra legem*, it can nonetheless be regarded, in the light of social development, as still only *praeter legem*, and as tacit law-making so as to effect a repeal. Aquinas' conclusion is that custom can interpret law, can abrogate it, and can also establish new law.[22]

This argument, it is suggested, remains a correct picture of how custom can develop law beyond, and eventually contrary to, a codifying instrument. It is the increasing number of cases in which the codified law "does not fit", in which it is natural and proper to apply a different rule, which eventually gives the new rule the status of law enabling it to over-ride the codified law, on the general principle that *lex posterior derogat priori*. The same problem, in modern terms, has been very clearly stated – and resolved in no substantially different manner – by Sir Gerald Fitzmaurice in his Hague lectures.[23]

Thus there can be little doubt that law deriving from the

legem agere, male fecit; ergo multiplicatis similibus actibus non efficietur aliquod bonum: lex autem est quoddam bonum, cum sit regula humanorum actuum; ergo per consuetudinem non potest removeri lex, ut ipsa consuetudo vim legis obtineat".

21. (Author's translation) "Leges humanae in aliquibus casibus deficiunt; unde possibile est quandoque praeter legem agere, in casu scilicet in quo deficit lex; et tamen actus non erit malus: et cum tales casus multiplicantur propter aliquam mutationem hominum, tunc manifestatur per consuetudinem. quod lex ulterius non est utilis; sicut etiam manifestaretur, si lex contraria verbo promulgaretur".

22. *Summa*, loc. cit.; quoted by Mateesco, *La coutume dans les cycles juridiques internationaux* (1947), p. 74.

23. 92 *Recueil des Cours*, 1957-II, at pp. 113-114.

provisions of a multilateral codifying treaty can be modified by a subsequent general practice constitutive of international custom.[24] However, general practice presupposes identity, or near-identity, of the parties to the original treaty and the "parties" to the subsequent variant custom: the problem becomes more complex when there is divergence of practice among the parties to the treaty, or when the original treaty was concluded among a limited group of States.

To take the second hypothesis first, what is the effect on a codifying treaty concluded on a regional level of a change in the customary law, applicable both within and without the region concerned by the treaty, which the codifying treaty had "photographed" (to use Professor Baxter's expression[25]) at an earlier stage in its development? The answer must depend, in the first place on the nature of the development which has occurred, and in the second place on whether the States parties to the treaty participated in the creation of the developed rule of custom. If the new rule is a matter of *jus cogens*, then to that extent it must clearly-over-ride the earlier regional treaty. If however it is simply a matter of *jus dispositivum* – which is more likely, since the rule which it replaces must *ex hypothesi* have been a matter of *jus dispositivum*, or regarded as such, to have found a place in a treaty – then the parties to the treaty will remain committed to the rule in the treaty unless they themselves have evinced an intention to discard it in favour of the new rule by participating in the creation of the custom. As between a treaty-rule and a rule of general international law, the treaty-rule, as *lex specialis*, must prevail, notwithstanding the fact that the general rule has developed since the treaty. If the parties to our hypothetical regional codification treaty have participated in the formation of the new customary rule, the situation is the same as that in which the codification, and the new custom, are both general in scope, which is the question next to be considered.

The hypothesis now is therefore, that a comparatively large number of States – practically the "generality" of States – have

24. Such a practice could be classified as simultaneously desuetude of the treaty and creation of customary law. On desuetude see McNair, *Law of Treaties*, pp. 516-518; J. Leca, *Les techniques de révision des conventions internationales* (1961) pp. 261ff.

25. Multilateral Treaties as Evidence of Customary International Law, 41 *B.Y.I.L.* (1965-66), p. 275 at p. 299. See above p. 126.

concluded and ratified, or acceded to, a codifying treaty; subsequently a practice springs up among a number of the States parties to the treaty which is in formal conflict with the terms of the treaty. It is to be supposed that if the treaty had never existed, the practice would, on the usual tests of regularity, consistency and existence of *opinio juris*, have been eligible for consideration as a new rule of customary law; what is the effect of the existence of the treaty on the legal significance of the practice?

It is tempting to assimilate the establishment of a custom conflicting with the terms of a multilateral treaty to the conclusion of a subsequent inconsistent treaty between some only of the parties to the original treaty. But there is a difficulty here: it will be recalled that the general rule for the revision or amendment of multilateral treaties is that the consent of all the parties to the original treaty is required. Is the establishment, or purported establishment, of a new rule of customary law in conflict with the provisions of a codifying treaty to be regarded as an amendment of the treaty or as an *inter se* modification as regards some only of its parties?

In general, a rule of customary international law, once it has become such a rule at all, operates with binding force on all States, and not merely those which have agreed to it or participated in its formation. There is however a certain awkwardness in regarding the specific and expressly accepted obligations and rights of a State under a treaty as over-ridden by a new customary rule in the elaboration of which that State took no part; it is difficult to reconcile the view that the growth of a subsequent general custom in the same matter over-rides the provisions of a treaty with the distinction between *jus cogens* and *jus dispositivum*.

The Vienna Convention on the Law of Treaties provides in Article 64 that

> "If a new *peremptory* norm of general international law emerges, any existing treaty which is in conflict with that norm becomes void and terminates."

This provision is of course primarily designed to operate with regard to bilateral treaties or plurilateral treaties not of a codifying type, but it must be applicable equally, if the situation arises, to codifying treaties. Thus some distinction must exist between new customary rules which over-ride existing treaties, even multilateral codifying treaties, with which they are in conflict, and rules of customary law which do not do so. The problem is that of the presumed universality of custom, and the potential, if not actual, universality or near-universality of acceptance of such treaties. It does not appear possible to resort to the argument that treaties create *lex specialis* between the parties, just invoked with regard to the position of parties to *local* codifying treaties, because it is difficult to argue that the law of the treaty is *lex specialis* when it was originally widely if not universally applied, and has now been discarded by a considerable number of the parties to the treaty.

If, on the other hand the subsequent practice of only some of the States parties to the treaty is to be regarded as binding upon those States only, there is some difficulty in regarding the new rule as one of customary law, or at least of general customary law; it may however be possible to consider it as a rule of special or local customary law.

It will thus be convenient at this point to examine briefly the particular problems raised by what is known as local (or regional, or special) customary law, and by codification carried on at other than an universal level. Up to this point we have, in general, only discussed codification on the basis that it will be, or at least will be intended to be, universally effective, so as to regulate the relations of all the States of the world; and even in the case of a convention which is only a codifying convention in the broad sense, which will be bound to pass through what may prove to be a lengthy intermediate period during which only the States parties to the convention will be bound by the rules set out therein, these States will probably be drawn from all quarters of the globe, and united only by their acceptance of the convention. This approach to the question of codification has been justified in as much as the trend today is towards codification on a world scale, and away from regional codification. It is paradoxical that whereas the battle fought by Alvarez[26] in the early years of the present century to secure recognition of a system of customary international law peculiar to the American continent has been won,[27] and – as we have noted[28] – the process of sub-division of international law is

26. On the controversy between Alvarez and Vianna on the law of the Americas, see, for example, Moreno Quintana, *Tratado de derecho internacional,* Vol. I, pp. 63-66.

27. The Judgments of the I.C.J. in the *Asylum* and *Right of Passage* cases may be said to have set the seal of respectability on local custom.

28. See above, p. 4.

accelerating as a result of the ideological and economic cleavages between States, and the feelings of local unity of the recently enfranchised African and Asian States, yet, at the same time, local codes, as opposed to asserted local law of customary origin, are less frequently proposed.[29]

The limitations on sovereignty successfully effected by the Treaty of Rome within the limited sphere of the European Economic Community may be taken as an indication that the establishment of a true international legislature is more likely to be achieved at a regional level than a universal one. Nevertheless, in the present state of development of international relations, local codification must be taken to rely on codifying treaties, supplemented by the effect of custom, to give it formal validity as law, just as in the case of universal codification.

The concept of local custom, although it has been a factor in several cases before the International Court of Justice, has never been as precisely defined as would be desirable. It is suggested that the vital question, which is unfortunately not treated at any length in one of the two principal recent studies of the subject,[30] [and taken as point of departure in the other,[31]] is that whether local custom is binding only on those States which have expressly agreed to it or accepted it, or may also be binding, in the same way as is general customary law, on other States members of the limited international community within which the local custom operates, but which have neither expressly accepted nor consistently protested against it from the time of its formation.

Considered from the point of view of the nature and effects of the codification process in international law, the problem is as follows. Within a certain defined region, a codification treaty is prepared and accepted by all or most of the members of the community of States. It may be remarked in passing that whereas in matters of local customary law in general it may often be difficult to ascertain exactly what are the boundaries of the "community" to which the custom in question is to be treated as applying, the problem is simplified if a convention is prepared, since *prima facie* States which participate in the preparation of the

29. The Addis Abbaba Charter is more of a constitutional document.

30. G. Cohen-Jonathan, La coutume locale, *Annuaire français* 1961, p. 119.

31. [A. d'Amato, The Concept of Special Custom in International Law, 63 *A.J.I.L.*, 1969, p. 211.]

convention may be taken to be members of the regional community. Are the rules expressed in the convention capable of applying to the States members of the local community which do not ratify the convention, on the basis either that they represented local customary law prior to the conclusion of the convention or that they have become so since, by practice including the ratification of the convention by other States? Either of these two processes are, as we have seen,[32] perfectly possible in the case of rules of general customary law, because there is no doubt that general customary law binds States which have not expressly accepted it.

In the *Asylum* case in 1950, the International Court of Justice, when discussing the institution of asylum in Latin America, made the following observations:

> "The Colombian Government has finally invoked 'American international law in general'. In addition to the rules arising from agreements which have already been considered, it has relied on an alleged regional or local custom peculiar to Latin-American States.
> The Party which relies on a custom of this kind must prove that this custom is established in such a manner that it has become binding on the other Party. The Colombian Government must prove that the rule invoked by it is in accordance with a constant and uniform usage practised by the States in question, and that this usage is the expression of a right . . . and a duty . . .".[33]

For a number or writers, the reference in the second paragraph quoted to "a constant and uniform usage practised by *the States in question*" signifies that in the view of the International Court a local custom is only opposable to States which actually participate in the practice giving rise to it, and not to any other States members of the community in which the custom arises.[34] The present writer does not share this view: it would seem that the

32. See above, p. 81ff.
33. *I.C.J. Reports 1950*, p. 266, at p. 276.
34. [This was asserted by the Federal Republic of Germany in the *Continental* Shelf cases (*I.C.J. Pleadings, Oral Arguments, Documents,* Vol. I, p. 60, para. 59) and accepted by Judge Ammoun (*I.C.J. Reports 1969*, pp. 130-131); the Court however did not deal with the point, since Denmark and the Netherlands had not argued on the basis of a regional or local custom, but on the basis of a general customary rule: *I.C.J. Pleadings, Oral Arguments, Documents*, Vol. I, pp. 196-7 and 350.] In this sense also, Verdross, Das völkerrechtliche Gewohnheitsrecht, 7 *Japanese Annual of International Law* (1963) p. 7, and *Völkerrecht,* p. 142, text and footnote; Sereni, *Diritto internazionale,* p. 130; Moreno Quintana, *Tratado de derecho internacional,* Vol. I, p. 72. Contra: Accioly, *Tratado de direito internacional público,* pp. 39-40.

reference to "the States in question" may have been deliberately imprecise, so as to avoid committing the Court further than necessary to the decision of the case;[35] it would have been more natural, if what was meant was that actual participation or consent was necessary, to say "practised by the Respondent among others". Furthermore, the Court proceeded to discuss the relevance of the Montevideo Convention, which had not been ratified by the Respondent (Peru), as evidence of State practice, which seems to assume that if sufficiently widespread State practice among Latin-American States could have been proved (e.g. by quasi-universal acceptance of the Montevideo Convention, or otherwise), the custom might have been opposable to Peru, presumably as a Latin-American State and a member of the community within which asylum as a concept existed, notwithstanding the absence of proof of acceptance of the custom claimed by Colombia, by ratification of the Montevideo Convention or otherwise, by Peru.

The view that local custom is binding only on States which have expressly agreed to it is fundamentally an assertion of the view that custom is based upon acceptance, the equation of custom with *pactum tacitum* associated in particular with the name of Strupp.[36] The view is obviously more defensible with regard to local custom than with regard to universal custom, since local custom is, of its nature, in no need of the support of all States. Thus the problem of States which express their dissent, or fail to express their assent, contemporaneously is less of a difficulty; but there remains the problem of new States.

It is suggested, in fact, that States which actively oppose a local custom are not bound by it, it being easier in this connection to establish "exclusion by historic title" *à la* Norway[37] than with regard to general law; that States which can be regarded as members of a community, either a geographical region or a community of interest, within which the custom has emerged, and which do not actively oppose the custom, are bound by it; and that new States coming into existence after the crystallisation of the custom are bound by it if they must be regarded as having been born into

35. Lauterpacht, *The Development of International Law by the International Court of Justice,* p. 75; cf. Ammoun in *I.C.J. Reports 1970,* p. 301.

36. Règles générales de la paix, 47 *Recueil des Cours*, 1934-I, p. 263ff.

37. See the reference to the *Fisheries* case above, p. 110.

the regional community to which it relates, as well as into the community of nations generally.[38] For example, new States which can be regarded as successors of States which were bound by the local custom must take the law of the region as they find it, just as they must take the law of the general international community as they find it.

[This view is supported by the decision of the International Court in the case concerning the *Right of Passage over Indian Territory*;[39] in that case, Portugal was asserting against India rights deriving from a bilateral local custom, but the practice on the basis of which the Court was able to find that such a custom existed was the practice of India's predecessors in title, the Marathas and the British Government in India, since during the period from Indian independence up to 1954 when the dispute arose, each side had reserved its legal position.[40] The question was of course complicated by the existence of treaties to which India had admittedly succeeded, and the customary rights had become, as it were, grafted on to the treaty rights, but nonetheless the decision of the Court was in effect that a local custom was binding on a State which had succeeded to the custom though it had not itself expressly consented thereto.

Even where a local custom is incapable of reciprocal application – the Portugese right of passage again being an example – the benefit of a local custom will only belong to the members of the relevant community, including their successors. Here again there may be some difficulty in determining the exact limits of the

38. [A contrary view has been expressed by Professor Zemanek, who admits the opposability of customary rules to States whose express consent thereto has not been demonstrated only if the rule has arisen within a juridically posited community (*rechtlich vorgegebene Gemeinschaft*) of States, and does not consider that even close bonds of a cultural, political or economic nature suffice to create such a community (Die Bedeutung der Kodifizierung des Völkerrechts für seine Anwendung, in *Festschrift Verdross*, p. 565 at p. 578). It is not clear whether the only community which meets this requirement is the international community as a whole; it may be that Professor Zemanek would resolve the problem of application of local custom to successor States by regarding the establishment of a local custom as creating a juridically postulated community comprising the consenting States, into which a successor to a consenting State would enter on its appearance.]

39. [*I.C.J. Reports 1960*, p. 6.]

40. [*I.C.J. Reports 1960* at p. 34: "It is clear from the material placed before the Court that before 1954, passage was effected in a way recognized as acceptable to both sides. Certain incidents occurred, but they did not lead the Parties to adopt clearly-defined legal positions as against each other".]

community: in the *Rights of U.S. Nationals in Morocco* case,[41] the existence of some customary rights of consular jurisdiction in the French zone of Morocco was proved, and the question was essentially whether the United States, which enjoyed similar rights by the effect of a most-favoured-nation clause combined with treaties conferring consular jurisdiction, was entitled to enjoy such rights after the disappearance of the treaties by virtue of the local custom, i.e. whether the United States was within the relevant "community"; and the Court's decision was that the fact that it had at all material times enjoyed treaty rights prevented it from benefiting from the customary rights.]

Finally, it is clear from the passage from the Judgment in the *Asylum* case quoted above that in the view of the International Court there is something of a presumption against rules of local customary law, so that the State which invokes such a rule will have to prove that it exists and is opposable to the State against which it is invoked. In cases where the alleged custom is purely bilateral, such as the *Right of Passage over Indian Territory* case just quoted, to prove that the custom exists at all will be sufficient, but in other cases some degree of proof of opposability will be demanded.

To return to the question of a new rule of customary law of limited acceptance conflicting with the provisions of a general codifying treaty, the argument just outlined does enable us to form a conclusion as to the effect of such a situation on the legal relationships involved. An established usage contrary to the treaty will, if the necessary requirements of consistency and *opinio juris* are satisfied, give rise to a rule of local customary law in derogation from the treaty-rules, applicable only to the States which have expressly or tacitly accepted it, or can be regarded as linked in a geographical or other community with the States which have established the custom, unless such fellow-members of the community have actively opposed the custom.

With reference to the question of the extent of the "community" subject to local customary rules, the term "local" custom, preferred by M. Cohen-Jonathan,[42] may be somewhat mis-

41. [*I.C.J. Reports 1952,* p. 176; discussed above, p. 92.]

42. La coutume locale, *Annuaire français 1961,* p. 119. [The International Court has used the terms "local" or "regional" custom (see *Wolfke, Custom in Present International Law*, p. 89); Professor d'Amato prefers the term "special custom": see The

leading. The terms is used only to indicate a rule of customary origin which is not applicable universally to all States; it does not imply any necessary precondition of geographical relationship. It might in fact be objected that it has never been clearly established that a rule of local custom can exist otherwise than between States forming a group united either by their being members of a defined geographical region, or by some common special circumstance, not applicable to other States: the model example of the first type of group being the States of Latin America, and a convenient example of the second group being States of differing geographical positions united by enjoying – by custom, and not by virtue of a treaty – parallel rights under the regime of capitulations in a given territory.[43] [Thus, in the view recently expressed by d'Amato,

> "*special* customary international law deals with non-generalizable topics such as title to or rights in specific portions of world real estate (e.g., cases of acquisitive prescription, boundary disputes, and so-called international servitudes), or with rules expressly limited to countries of a certain region (such as the law of asylum in Latin America)."[44]]

If the only link between a number of States is that they agree in preferring a particular rule, which they have developed by application in practice, to a different rule governing the same point, laid down in a general codifying treaty, can this identity or similarity of practice, possibly in widely separated areas of the world, be regarded as a custom at all, even a "local" or "special" custom?

However, it must be borne in mind that every practice which is of any relevance in international law must, in principle, have two sides to it: that is to say the active practice of one State or subject of international law must be such as to affect the rights or interests of other States or other subjects of international law, so as to place the latter in a position where they must decide between tacitly agreeing to the activities of the other State, or objecting to

---

Concept of Special Custom in International Law, 63 *A.J.I.L.*, 1969, pp. 211ff., and *The Concept of Custom in International Law*, pp. 233ff.]

43. Cf. the *Rights of American Nationals in Morocco* case, *I.C.J. Reports 1952*, p. 176.

44. [The Concept of Special Custom in International Law, 63 *A.J.I.L.* (1969), p. 211, at pp. 212-3. Verdross on the other hand speaks of special customary law arising within a "Kulturkreis" – presumably not necessarily, though normally, geographically delimited (Das völkerrechtliche Gewohnheitsrecht, 7 *Japanese Annual of International Law*, 1963, at p. 7). Cf. Zemanek's requirement of a "rechtlich vorgebene Gemeinschaft": supra, note 38.]

it. We have already observed the operation of this principle in connection with international legislation in matters normally forming part of the reserved domain, and have noted the difficulty to which it gives rise in connection with the view that ratifications of codifying treaties may amount to acts of State practice.

In the situation now under consideration, the divergent practice of some of the States parties to a codifying convention cannot be regarded as wholly disjointed, even if the States *actively* following the practice are geographically widely separated, and not linked by a common and direct special interest in the subject-matter of the convention. If States A, M and X, in different continents, adopt the same practice (which is in conflict with the rules laid down in a codifying convention to which they are all parties), it must be supposed that their action will call for some reaction from States B and C, N and O, and Y and Z, their neighbours – since if the practice affects no-one but the State adopting it, it is not eligible for consideration as a custom in any event.[45] Assuming that the "neighbour" States do not object to the practice, one may speak of a local custom arising between A,B and C, and the same custom – or a separate but similar custom – arising between M,N and O, and between X,Y and Z. Thus the requirement of a "local community" within which the local custom is framed, is satisfied; but it should again be emphasised that it would also be satisfied if the connection between A, B and C were not geographical but of some other kind.

It also emerges from our discussion of the nature of local customary law that, since local customary law, even on a wide scale, is not binding on States which have not accepted it and are not part of the "community" to which it relates, variations of a regime laid down by a codifying treaty which come into existence only between certain States or groups of States will be more akin to a *modification* of the original treaty than to an amendment or revision thereof. Since however general international customary

45. [The effective acceptance of merely *one* other State will suffice to create a customary rule; as the International Court observed in the *Right of Passage* case, "It is difficult to see why the number of States between which a local custom may be established on the basis of long practice must necessarily be larger than two" (*I.C.J. Reports 1960*, p. 39). However, in such a case the consent of the other State will normally have to be clearly proved; the "local community" test suggested above will only be capable of application with regard to successor States; cf. Guggenheim, Lokales Gewohnheitsrecht. *Öster. Ztschr. für Öff. Recht*, XI, 1961, at p. 330.]

law does not require the consent of all States to become binding on the whole international community, but only the consent of the "generality" of States, it may in some instances prove difficult to draw the dividing line between a modification of a codified regime which operates as a very widespread local custom and a new rule of general international law of customary origin. But until the existence of a rule of general law amending the treaty can be clearly established, the treaty regime will continue to exist unabated for such States as have neither accepted the new customary rule, nor been or become members of the community to which it applies; and this again will tend to produce a situation of divergence or diversity of legal relationships and practice in a field which it will presumably have been one of the objects of the codifying treaty to unify.

We may round off this Chapter devoted to consideration of the state of international law subsequent to the conclusion of a codifying treaty by touching briefly on another point of difficulty which is foreseeable with regard to such treaties. At the outset of this study, we drew attention to the great increase in the number of States forming the international community, largely as a result of the process of emancipation of numerous territories of Africa and Asia which were formerly subject to Mandate, or international trusteeship, or were otherwise dependent and therefore not counted as sovereign members of the community. This is a process which must have its natural end sooner or later, and in fact the number of territories capable of becoming self-governing entities which still remain in some sort of dependent status is very considerably reduced.

Nevertheless, it must be assumed for the future that new States will continue to emerge from time to time, either as this process completes itself, or as a result of the division of existing States, or of other political changes. Therefore the question of what law is binding upon new States will continue to have a considerable amount of importance.

For general customary law, the problem is not new, and must be regarded as solved in the sense that, subject to the possible impact of the disapproval of blocs of newly emerged States, resulting in a change in the law, discussed in our first Chapter, the whole of general customary law will be applicable to new States.

But as between the law expressed in codifying treaties, on the one hand, and divergent practice on the other, there may be some considerable difficulty in coming to a conclusion as to what the rights and obligations of a new State are to be. In many cases, it may be possible to apply the "local community" test suggested above, but it cannot be pretended that such a test will necessarily be accepted in all cases, nor that it will always be easy to apply. A certain amount of uncertainty seems likely to subsist at least so long as the new State has not made its position known, e.g. by declaring its adherence to the general treaty, [by acceding thereto or giving notice that it regards the treaty as continuing to apply to itself,] and thereby allying itself to the system laid down therein.

Such adherence will, it is suggested, be necessary for the application of the treaty to the new State to be placed beyond doubt. In so far as it is to be applied as a treaty, and not as evidence of pre-existing or subsequently established customary law, the question is one of succession – a question of notorious difficulty and controversy.[46] So far as "law-making" treaties are concerned, the problem has been the subject of a detailed examination by Dr. Jenks,[47] whose conclusion, after studying doctrine, practice and international case-law, was that the matter was an open question. It does not appear that since 1952 the matter has become so much clearer as to warrant any definite statement as to the position of new States under codifying treaties.

To the extent that such treaties enact, state or crystallise general international customary law, there is no problem of theory. But it is open to a new State to attemtp to dispute, first that the treaty ever represented general law – a question which may or may not be easy to resolve according to the other evidence available – and second that the law has developed since the treaty was concluded: and here, in the light of our examination of the process of development by custom, the claim may be on safe ground, or at least on ground which it will be very difficult to shake. Thus in this connection also, codification may sometimes prove to have been the purchase of immediate consistency and order at the price of later difficulty and divergence.

46. [A copious bibliography will be found in O'Connell, Independence and Succession to Treaties, 38 *B.Y.I.L.* (1962) at p. 85, footnote 1, and the same author's *The Law of State Succession*.]

47. State Succession in respect of Law-Making Treaties, 29 *B.Y.I.L.* (1952), p. 105.

Chapter Ten

CONCLUSION

Having come to the end of our examination of the role which custom can play in the present period of codification of international alw, we may now endeavour briefly to sum up some of the conclusions that emerge from it.

It is not for us to dwell on the merits and de-merits of codification in the international field: its merits have been sufficiently stressed by more able authors, and both merits and de-merits have been well ventilated in the discussions of the International Law Commission, the discussions in the General Assembly upon the Reports of the Commission, and the commentaries of legal writers on the work of the Commission generally. It is however hoped that we have been able to draw attention to some of the less obvious difficulties and diasadvantages to which the continuing codification movement may sometimes lead.

We have endeavoured to emphasise the need to keep in mind the way in which international law actually lends its force to norms which arise either out of practice or out of the proposals of statesmen – in treaties of traditional type – or of legal scholars. Only by way of treaty or of general acceptance as law can such norms acquire effective existence. There is here a difficulty which is fundamental in the present state of development of international society. Since States are their own lawmakers, the only way in which law can become truly universal, so as to bind even those States which have not formally effected some act of acceptance of it, is by acceptance by the generality of States and incorporation into international customary law. But the essence of customary law is that it is *lex non-scripta*, and that it is frequently disorderly and often uncertain. But in the absence – which is likely to continue for many years yet – of a true legislature on the international level, the *lex scripta*, which can be precise, clear and orderly, cannot, as *lex scripta*, be universal.

Thus the universal law is incomplete and disordered; the ordered and complete law cannot be universal. But one must not, as we have seen, exaggerate the seriousness of the practical problems involved, and lose sight of the question, What is international law for? In the post-war world, the objects of law are surely closely identified with the objects set out in Article 1 of the Charter of the United Nations, and in particular

> "To maintain international peace and security, and to that end . . . to bring about by peaceful means . . . adjustment or settlement of international disputes or situations which might lead to a breach of the peace. . .

It would be a mistake to under-rate the part that customary law plays, and will continue to play, in achieving these ends, merely because many problems of law – particularly of "lawyers' law" – do not find in general international custom any clear and definite answer.

We have seen that an international legislature, though it does not yet exist and cannot be expected to be established in the near future, is not an impossible concept: that the sources of law can and will vary and develop with the development of the international community. At the same time, we must be on our guard against allowing the desirability of a given development to blind us to the obstacles it will have to overcome, and against assuming that they have been overcome. In particular, it is clear that no new source of law can come to exist except through the operation of the law flowing from one of the existing and recognised sources.

To appreciate the role of custom in the present and future international community, one must form a clear idea of what custom is and how it is formed. In particular, the existence of the two classic elements in its formation, the material element of usage and the psychological element of the *opinio juris*, must be insisted on as a pre-condition for recognition of any rule or principle which presents itself under the banner of international custom.

The nature of the two constitute elements in custom may also develop, provided development does not become distortion from the essential nature of custom. It is doubtful whether classical theory would have regarded the mere act of the ratifying a multilateral treaty as an act of State practice capable of contributing to the conversion of the rules set out in the treaty into customary law; but this development has the sanction of the International Court of Justice, and is, it is suggested, consistent with the nature of custom. On the other hand, a mere statement of what is understood to be the law, let alone a mere affirmative vote cast by a State representative in favour of such a statement cannot be regarded as having sufficient of the concrete, self-committing, character which markes State practice formative of international custom.

As to the *opinio juris*, we have attempted to show to some extent the effect which differing concepts of this most elusive aspect of custom may have on the relationship of custom with codified law, and we have allied ourselves with a view which is basically that of Rachel:

> "Jus igitur gentium est jus, plurium liberarum gentium pacto sive placito expresse aut tacite initum quo *utilitatis gratia* sibi invicem obligantur".[1]

Finally we have endeavoured to show that so far from supplanting customary law, and reducing its field of operation to a minimum, the codifying of great tracts of international law will, on account of the practical and political difficulties of amending multilateral treaties, whether codifying or otherwise, give over the development of international law almost entirely into the hands of custom, operating upon and beyond the codifying treaties.

1. Rachel, Dissertatio de jure gentium (1676), Chapter XVI.

TABLE OF BOOKS AND ARTICLES CITED

Accioly, H.: Tratado de direito internacional público (Rio de Janeiro, 1956)

Ago, R.: La codification du droit international et les problèmes de sa réalisation, *Mélanges en hommage à Paul Guggenheim* (Faculté de droit de l'Université de Genève, 1968), p. 508

Allen, Sir Carleton K.: Law in the Making (Oxford, 1958)

Aquinas, St. Thomas: Summa Theologica (Rome edition, 1894)

Asamoah, O.Y.: The Legal Significance of the Declarations of the General Assembly of the United Nations (Nijhoff, The Hague, 1966)

Balladore Pallieri, G.: Diritto internazionale pubblico (6th ed, Giuffrè, Milan, 1952)

—: La forza obbligatoria della consuetudine internazionale, XX *Rivista di diritto internazionale* (1928), p. 338

Barberis, J.A.: L'élément matériel de la coutume internationale d'après la Cour de La Haye (1922-1966), XIV *Nederlands Tijdschrift* (1967) p. 367

—: L'*opinio juris* comme élément constitutif de la coutume d'après la Cour de La Haye, 50 *Rivista* (1967), p. 563

Basak, A.: Decisions of United Nations Organs in the Judgments and Opinions of the International Court of Justice (Warsaw, 1969)

Basdevant, J.: Règles générales de la paix, 54 *Recueil des cours*, 1936-IV, p. 508

—(ed.): Dictionnaire de la terminologie du droit international, (Sirey, Paris, 1960)

Bastid, S.: Observations sur une "étape" dans le développement progressif et la codification des principes du droit international, *Melanges en hommage à Paul Guggenheim* (Faculté de droit de l'Université de Genève, 1968), p. 132

Baxter, R.R.: Multilateral Treaties as Evidence of Customary International Law, 41 *B.Y.I.L.* (1965-66), p. 275

—: The effects of ill-conceived codification and development of international law, *Mélanges en hommage à Paul Guggenheim* (Faculté de droit de l'Université de Genève, 1968), p. 146

—: Treaties and Custom, 129 *Recueil des cours*, 1970-I, p. 31

Bishop, W.W.: Reservations to Treaties, 103 *Recueil des cours*, 1961-II, p. 249

Bleicher, S.A.: The Legal Significance of Re-Citation of General Assembly Resolutions, 63 *A.J.I.L.* (1969), p. 444

Bowett, D.W.: Estoppel before International Tribunals and its Relation to Acquiescence, 33 *B.Y.I.L.* (1957), p. 176

Briggs, H.W.: The International Law Commission (Cornell University Press, Ithaca, New York, 1965)

—: Reflections on the Codification of International Law by the International Law Commission and other Agencies, 126 *Recueil des cours*, 1969-I, p. 233

—: The Columbian-Peruvian Asylum case and Proof of International Customary Law, 45 *A.J.I.L.* (1951), p. 728

Carbonnier, J.: Droit civil (Collection Thémis, Paris, 1964)

Castañeda, J.: Legal Effects of United Nations Resolutions (Columbia University Press, 1969)

Cavaré, L.: Le droit international public positif (Pedone, Paris, 1967)

Cohen-Jonathan, G.: La coutume locale, *Annuaire français* 1961, p. 119

Cheng, Bin: Justice and Equity in International Law, *Current Legal Problems* 1955, p. 185

—: United Nations Resolutions on Outer Space: "Instant" International Customary Law? , V *Indian Journal of International Law* (1965), p. 23

d'Amato, A.: The Concept of Custom in International Law (Cornell University Press, 1971)

—: On Consensus, 8 *Canadian Yearbook of International Law*, 1970, p. 104

—: The Concept of Special Custom in International Law, 63 *A.J.I.L.* (1969), p. 211

—: The Authoritativeness of Custom in International Law, 53 *Rivista* 1970, p. 491

Darwin, H.G.: The Outer Space Treaty, 42 *B.Y.I.L.* (1967), p. 278

Degan, V.D.: L'Equité et le Droit International (Nijhoff, The Hague, 1970)
De Visscher, Ch.: La codification du droit international, 6 *Recueil des cours*, 1925-I, p. 325
—: Théories et réalités en droit international public (Pedone, Paris, 1955)
Duisberg, C.J.: Das subjektive Element im Völkergewohnheitsrecht unter besondere Berücksichtigung der Rechtsprechung des Ständigen Internationalen Gerichtshofs, 12 *Jahrbuch für Internationales Recht* (1965), p. 140
Ermacora, G.: Human Rights and Domestic Jurisdiction, 124 *Recueil des cours*, 1968-II, p. 371
Falk, R.A.: On the Quasi-legislative Competence of the General Assembly, 60 *A.J.I.L.* (1966), p. 782
Fenet: Recueil complet des travaux préparatoires du Code civil
Fitzmaurice, Sir Gerald G.: International Law from the Standpoint of the Rule of Law, 92 *Recueil des cours*, 1957-II, p.
—: Reports on the Law of Treaties for the International Law Commission, *I.L.C. Yearbooks* 1956-II, p. 104; 1957-II, p. 18; 1958-II, p. 27; 1959-II, p. 37; 1960-II, p. 69
—: Some Problems regarding the Formal Sources of International Law, *Symbolae Verzijl* (Nijhoff, The Hague, 1958), p. 153
Francois, J.P.A.: Handboek van het Volkenrecht (2nd. ed., 1947-50, Tjeenk Willink, Zwolle)
—: Grondlijnen van het Volkenrecht (3rd. ed., 1967, Tjeenk Willink, Zwolle)
Friedmann, W.: General Course in Public International Law, 127 *Recueil des cours* 1969-II, p. 39
Gianni, G.: La coutume en droit international (Paris, 1931)
Goedhuis, D.: Reflections on the Evolution of Space Law, XIII *Nederlands Tijdschrift* (1966), p. 109
—: The International Law Association and the Development of a Legal Regime of Outer Space, *New Frontiers in Space Law* (Sijthoff/Oceana, 1969), p. 31
Green, L.C.: De l'influence des nouveaux Etats sur le droit international, 74 *R.G.D.I.P.* (1970), p. 78
Grzybowski, K.: Soviet Public International Law (Sijthoff, Leyden, 1970)
Guggenheim, P.: Lehrbuch des Völkerrechts (Verlag für Recht und Gesellschaft, Basel, 1948-1951)

—: Les deux éléments de la coutume en droit international, *Etudes en l'honneur de Geroges Scelle*, Vol. I, p. 275

Günther, H.: Zur Entstehung von Völkergewohnheitsrecht (Berlin, 1970)

Hart, H.L.A.: The Concept of Law (Oxford, 1961)

Higgins, R.: The Development of International Law through the Political Organs of the United Nations (Oxford, 1963)

Hoyt, E.C.: The Unanimity Rule in the Revision of Treaties: A Re-examination (Nijhoff, The Hague, 1969)

Hudson, M.: International Legislation (Carnegie Endowment, Washington, 1931)

—: The Permanent Court of International Justice, 1920-1942 (Macmillan, New York, 1943)

Jenks, C.W.: State Succession in respect of Law-Making Treaties, 29 *B.Y.I.L.* (1952), p. 105

—: The Conflict of Law-Making Treaties, 30 *B.Y.I.L.* (1953), p. 401

—: The Prospects of International Adjudication (Stevens, London, 1964)

—: Space Law (Stevens, London, 1965)

—: A New World of Law? (Longmans, London, 1969)

Jennings, R.Y.: The Progress of International Law, 34 *B.Y.I.L.* (1958), p. 337

—: Recent Developments in the International Law Commission: its Relation to the Sources of International Law, *I.C.L.Q.* 1964, p. 385

—: General Course of International Law, 121 *Recueil des cours*, 1967-II, p. 323

Johnson, D.H.N.: The Conclusions of International Conferences, 35 *B.Y.I.L.* (1959), p. 1

Kelsen, H.: Théorie du droit international coutumier, *Revue internationale de la théorie du droit*, 1939, p. 253

Kopalmanas, L.: Custom as a Means of the Creation of International Law, 18 *B.Y.I.L.* (1937), p. 127

Krylov, B.: Codification du droit international, *Hommage d'une génération de juristes au président Basdevant* (Pedone, Paris, 1960), p. 314

Kunz, A.: The Nature of Customary International Law, 47 *A.J.I.L.* (1953), p. 662

—: The Present Status of the International Law for the Protection of Minorities, 48 *A.J.I.L.* (1954), p. 282

Lachs, M.: Recognition and Modern Methods of International Co-operation, 35 *B.Y.I.L.* (1959), p. 252

—: Le rôle des Organisations internationales dans la formation du droit international, *Mélanges Rolin* (Pedone, Paris, 1964), p. 157

—: The International Law of Outer Space, 113 *Recueil des cours*, 1964-III, p. 4

—: The Law-making Process for Outer Space, *New Frontiers in Space Law* (Sijthoff/Oceana, 1969), p. 13

Lang, J.: Le plateau continental de la Mer du Nord (Librairie générale, Paris, 1970)

Lauterpacht, Sir Hersch: Private Law Sources and Analogies of International Law (Longmans, London, 1927)

—: The Function of Law in the International Community (Oxford, Clarendon Press, 1933)

—: International Law and Human Rights (Stevens, London, 1950)

—: Reports on the Law of Treaties for the International Law Commission, *I.L.C. Yearbooks* 1953-II, p. 156; 1954-II, p. 133

—: Codification and Development of International Law, 49 *A.J.I.L.* (1955), p. 16

—: Collected Papers (ed. E. Lauterpacht) (Cambridge, 1970)

Leca, J.: Les techniques de révision des conventions internationales (Paris, 1961)

Machiavelli, N.: Il principe

MacGibbon, I.C.: Some Observations on the Part of Protest in International Law, *30 B.Y.I.L.* (1953), p. 293

—: Customary International Law and Acquiscence, 33 *B.Y.I.L.* (1957), p. 115

McNair, Lord: The Functions and Differing Legal Character of Treaties, 11 *B.Y.I.L.* (1930), p. 100

—: International Legislation, *XIX Iowa Law Review* (1934)

—: The Development of International Law (New York, 1954)

—: The Law of Treaties (Oxford, 1961)

McWhinney, E.: Le "nouveau" droit international et la "nouvelle" communauté mondiale, *R.G.D.I.P.* (1968), p. 323

Mateesco, N.: La coutume dans les cycles juridiques internationaux (Pedone, Paris, 1947)

Mokre, H.: Theorie des Gewohnheitsrechts (Springer, Vienna, 1932)

Morelli, G.: Nozioni di diritto internazionale (Padua, 1967)

Moreno Quintana, L.M.: Tratado de derecho internacional (Editorial sudamericana, Buenos Aires, 1963)

Mouton, M.W.: The Impact of Science on International Law, 119 *Recueil des cours*, 1966-III, p. 183

O'Connell, D.P.: International Law (Stevens, London, 1965)

Oppenheim: International Law, 5th edition by Hersch Lauterpacht (Longmans Green, London, 1937)

Quadri, R.: Droit international public, 113 *Recueil des cours*, 1964-III, p. 245

—: Diritto internazionale pubblico, (Liguore, Naples, 1968)

—: Le fondement du caractère obligatoire du droit international public, 80 *Recueil des cours*, 1952-I, p. 583

Rachel: Dissertatio de jure gentium, (1676), Classics of International Law, ed. von Bar (Washington, Carnegie Institute, 1916)

Ramos Galino, F.: Las resoluciones de la Asemblea General de las Naciones Unidas y su fuerza legal, XI *Revista Espanola de Derecho Internacional* (1958), p. 95

Reuter, P.: Institutions internationales (6th ed., Collection Thémis, Paris, 1969)

Ross, A.: A Textbook of International Law (Longmans Green, London, 1947)

Rousseau, Ch.: Droit international public (Paris, 1953)

Scelle, G.: Règles générales du droit de la paix, 46 *Recueil des cours*, 1933-IV, p. 327

—: Report on draft Convention on Arbitral Procedure, *I.L.C. Yearbook* 1957-II, p. 1

Schulz, G.: Entwicklungsformen internationaler Gesetzgebung (Göttingen, 1960)

Schwarzenberger, G.: A Manual of International Law (Stevens, London, 1967)

Sereni, A.P.: Diritto internazionale (Giuffrè, Milan, 1956)

—: I nuovi Stati ed il diritto internazinale, 50 *Rivista* (1967), p. 5

—: Les nouveaux Etats et le droit international, *R.G.D.I.P.* (1968) p. 305

Shihata, I.F.I.: The Treaty as a Law-Declaring and Custom-Making

Instrument, 22 *Revue égyptienne de droit international* (1966), p. 51

Siorat, L.: Le problème des lacunes en droit international (Librairie générale, Paris, 1958)

Skubiszewski, K.: Enactment of Law by International Organizations, 41 *B.Y.I.L.* (1965-66), p. 198

—: A New Source of the Law of Nations: Resolutions of International Organizations, *Mélanges en hommage à Paul Guggenheim* (Faculté de droit de l'Université de Genève, 1968), p. 508

Sørensen, M.: Les sources du droit international (Copenhagen, 1946)

—: Principes de droit international public, 101 *Recueil des cours,* 1960-III, p. 1

Steinicke, D.: Möglichkeiten einer Lösung des Theorienstreites über die Voraussetzungen der Gewohnheitsrechtsbildung im Völkerrecht, *Völkerrecht – Gewohnheitsrecht – Naturrecht* (Universität Hamburg, 1967)

Stone, J.: *Non liquet* and the Function of Law in the International Community, 35 *B.Y.I.L. (1959), p. 124*

Strupp, K.: Règles générales de la paix, 47 *Recueil des cours,* 1934-I, p. 263

Tunkin, G.: Co-existence and International Law, 95 *Recueil des cours,* 1958-II, p. 3

—: Remarks on the Juridical Nature of Customary Norms of International Law, *29 Cal. L.R.* (1961) p. 419

—: Droit international public (translation) (Pedone, Paris, 1965)

Vattel, E. de: Le droit des gens, ed. Pradier Fodéré (Guillermain et Cie., Paris, 1863)

Verdross, A.: Völkerrecht (5th ed., Vienna, 1964)

—: Das Völkerrechtliche Gewohnheitsrecht, 7 *Japanese Annual of International Law* (1963), p. 1

—: Kann die Generalversammlung der Vereinten Nationen das Völkerrecht weiterbilden?, XXVI *Zeitschrift* (1966), p. 690

Waldock, Sir Humphrey: General Course on Public International Law, 106 *Recueil des cours,* 1962-II, p. 1

—: Reports on the Law of Treaties for the International Law Commission, *I.L.C. Yearbooks* 1962-II, p. 160; 1963-II, p. 53; 1964-II, p. 5

Weber, H.: Das Völkergewohnheitsrecht aus der Sicht der Sowjetunion, *Völkerrecht – Gewohnheitsrecht – Naturrecht* (Universität Hamburg, 1967)

Weis, P.: The 1967 Protocol relating to the Status of Refugees and some Questions of the Law of Treaties, 42 *B.Y.I.L.* (1967), p. 40

Wolfke, K.: Custom in Present International Law (Warsaw Scientific Society, 1964)

Wright, Q.: Custom as a Basis for International Law in the Post-War World, 7 *Indiana Law Review,* p. 1

Zafrulla Khan, Sir Muhammad: The Contribution of the Principal Judicial Organ of the United Nations to the Achievement of the Objectives of the Organization, *U.N. Monthly Chronicle*, July 1970

Zemanek, K.: Die Bedeutung der Kodifizierung des Völkerrechts für seine Anwendung, *Internationale Festschrift für Alfred Verdross* (Wilhelm Fink, München-Salzburg, 1971), p. 565

Ziccardi, P.: La consuetudine internazionale nella teoria delle fonte giuridiche, *X Communicazioni e studi* (1958-9), p. 187

Žourek, J.: Report on the Law of Consular Intercourse and Immunities for the International Law Commission, *I.L.C. Yearbook* 1957-II, p. 71

INDEX